WIMBLEDON

WIMB

THE CHAMPIONSHIPS
WIMBLEDON

THE CHAMPIONSHIPS
WIMBLEDON

THE
CHAMPIONSHIPS
WIMBLEDON

Official Annual 1999

JOHN PARSONS

Photographs by
CLIVE BRUNSKILL, GARY M. PRIOR and ALEX LIVESEY
of Allsport Photographic

This first edition published in 1999 by Hazleton Publishing Ltd,
3 Richmond Hill, Richmond, Surrey TW10 6RE

ISBN: 1-874557-19-5

Printed in England by Ebenezer Baylis & Son Ltd, Worcester

Colour reproduction by Barrett Berkeley Ltd, London

Results tables are reproduced by courtesy of
The All England Lawn Tennis Club

This book is produced with the assistance of Canon

Publisher
RICHARD POULTER

Editor
JOHN PARSONS

Production Manager
STEVEN PALMER

Publishing Development Manager
SIMON MAURICE

Business Development Manager
SIMON SANDERSON

Art Editor
STEVE SMALL

Managing Editor
PETER LOVERING

Publicity and promotion
CLARE KRISTENSEN

Production Assistant
IMOGEN DALLEY

Photography
CLIVE BRUNSKILL
GARY M. PRIOR
ALEX LIVESEY
CLIVE MASON
PHIL COLE
STEPHEN MUNDAY

Photo Research, Allsport
ELAINE LOBO
KER ROBERTSON

FOREWORD

It is a pleasure to write the Foreword to this Annual, which records a remarkable fortnight of outstanding tennis. The quality of the tennis shone through from the first service on the first day, delivered by Pete Sampras, to the joyous end of the mixed doubles late on the final Sunday. All the excitement and pleasure of The Championships is captured in this annual as a lasting memory.

During the first week Boris Becker pleased his many loyal fans with his continuing success at Wimbledon, while Jim Courier followed his Davis Cup triumph against Great Britain by displaying his mental strength with tough five-set wins over Carlos Moya and Sjeng Schalken. There was also the shock of the tournament in the first round, when Jelena Dokic beat Martina Hingis, and we saw the emergence of other young stars in the ladies' singles.

In the second week the fans had the pleasure of Tim Henman's five-set triumph against Jim Courier, the athleticism of Pat Rafter, and the unbelievable dynamism of Andre Agassi. With the ladies we enjoyed the continuing success of the youngsters who had come through the first week – Jelena Dokic, Alexandra Stevenson and Mirjana Lucic. The ladies' quarter-final between Venus Williams and Steffi Graf was outstanding – a match that reached the height of excellence, particularly in the third set, which more than made up for the many interruptions caused by rain.

The final weekend was a triumph over the weather difficulties experienced earlier in the week. We were rewarded on the Sunday by the confirmation of Lindsay Davenport as a player of real quality – the completeness of her game and penetration of her shots had carried all before her throughout the two weeks, and the final was no exception. The success of Leander Paes and his partners in the men's doubles and mixed doubles was an added bonus. But the lasting memory for tennis fans from that wonderful Sunday has to be the awesome grass-court tennis played by Pete Sampras. Andre Agassi played well, but Pete was not to be denied and put himself in the record books in many ways – six Wimbledon Championships in the last seven years, 12 Grand Slams, and a consistent quality of tennis never seen before.

I hope you enjoy this Annual, and that it will provide you with a glimpse and reminder of a great Championships – the last of the century.

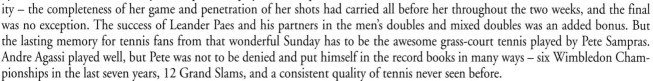

John Curry
Chairman of The All England Lawn Tennis & Croquet Club
and the Committee of Management of The Championships

INTRODUCTION

SELDOM since the days of Fred Perry's dominance had there been such a genuine feeling of expectation that, after 63 years, another British player could win the men's singles at Wimbledon. Tim Henman, 24, and Greg Rusedski, 25, were both at a stage of their careers when it was reasonable to suppose they were close to their peaks, when perhaps, on the evidence of the first six months of the year, Pete Sampras, still the top-seeded favourite, might just have passed his.

Both had demonstrated in the past how well their games are suited to grass, but they were drawn in the same half so, if it came down to that, one of them certainly was going to be disappointed. Yet hopes and dreams are one thing. Reality can so often prove to be entirely different and the most vital question needing to be asked before the fortnight began was a familiar one: 'Who will beat Sampras?'

Rusedski had demonstrated on an indoor court in Paris the previous November that he could. Henman drew sufficient confidence from his recent defeat against the American at Queen's Club, effectively decided by one missed overhead, to believe that he, too, was ready to do so.

Yet that Stella Artois title, his first for eight months, was perfectly timed music to the American's ears and whatever his unimpressive record hitherto during the year, as John McEnroe,

who knows a thing or two about the game, said, Sampras becomes so inspired once he steps on to the Wimbledon grass that he could probably take the rest of the year off and still have a great chance of being the champion.

Sampras, as ever, played it cool. There was far more at stake for him than merely being successful in defending the title. If he did so, he would become the first player since the abolition of The Challenge Round, whereby the winner one year did not have to risk his title until the final the next, to become champion for a sixth time. It would also be his 12th Grand Slam title, equalling the all-time record held by Roy Emerson. 'I'm not setting any particular dates for particular targets,' said Sampras in his typical low-key fashion. 'If it happens, it happens. I'll just be doing my best to make it happen.'

Take away the crucial Sampras factor and the men's singles at Wimbledon '99 had been looking about as open as most could recall in recent years, even before the stunning finals in the French Open, which further muddied the waters of prediction, for both the men and the ladies. Suddenly, just when most had imagined that Andre Agassi's and Steffi Graf's glory days would persist only in the record books, both not only came from behind to win spectacular finals at Roland Garros, but also were clearly hungry and committed to do more.

Agassi's sole Wimbledon triumph had been seven distant

years earlier, and less than two years ago, when his interest, as well as his world ranking (141), had slumped, few would have gambled on such a swift and spectacular renaissance. Steffi Graf's victory was her first in a Grand Slam since 1996, since when injuries had inevitably continued to provoke more forecasts about a possible retirement than her becoming a rejuvenated champion.

When the draw, with a little help from the seeding committee in the ladies' singles, made it possible for Martina Hingis to have to face Graf again in one final and for there to be a classic all-American confrontation between Sampras and Agassi in the other, it all added to the growing list of fascinating possibilities ahead. And that was taking only the most obvious candidates for success into account.

On the men's side, one could never discount Goran Ivanisevic at Wimbledon. In 1998, after barely a victory of substance along the way, he had reached the final and with his serve he would be quite capable of doing so again. Similarly the Dutchman, Richard Krajicek, had given notice when winning the Lipton title in March that he was already focusing on trying to repeat his Wimbledon success in 1996. Mark Philippoussis too, with signs that his game was maturing into something more than a serving rocket-launcher, was likely to be a threat to most people, while there was a strong feeling that his more experienced fellow Australian, Patrick Rafter, might at last be ready to overcome his fears about not being able to move well on grass.

Most views about the ladies' singles leant towards the theory that, after the way her tennis and her self-control had slipped in the Roland Garros final, Martina Hingis would be even more determined to win the only Grand Slam title that still eluded her. A final between her and either Graf or the heavy-hitting Venus Williams seemed to be the favoured choice, especially as Jana Novotna's ankle injury in Paris seemed to have ended any real chance of her keeping the title.

What no one knew, though, before the tournament began, was the full magnitude of the post-Paris emotional stress Hingis was under. Nor was there a true appreciation of the extent to which Mirjana Lucic and above all qualifiers Jelena Dokic and Alexandra Stevenson could add to the threat already posed by fellow teenagers, Williams and Anna Kournikova, or the thoroughness with which Lindsay Davenport had been preparing on grass.

You can find out here as the dramatic events of Wimbledon '99 are recorded in words and pictures in the pages that follow.

Opposite: Canons at the ready. The cream of the world's sports photographers capture the thrilling action and the unique atmosphere that is Wimbledon.

Below: Double delight on Independence Day as Lindsay Davenport and Pete Sampras proudly display their trophies.

Canon

IT'S PLAYED FOR THIS

T IT'S WON WITH THIS

POTENTIAL.

IT'S THERE TO

BE REALISED

 Canon is proud to be an Official Supplier to The Championships, Wimbledon.
http://sport.canon-europa.com

pete SAMPRAS

pat RAFTER

Pete Sampras (United States)
Age: 27
Born: Washington DC
World ranking: 1

Pat Rafter (Australia)
Age: 26
Born: Mount Isa, Queensland
World ranking: 2

Ever since Pete Sampras won the title for the first of five times in 1993, all his peers knew that, on the grass at Wimbledon, he was the one they had to beat. He went into the last Wimbledon of the millennium having won 39 of his previous 40 matches at the tournament. Only Richard Krajicek, who went on to win the title in 1996, had beaten him.

Yet, after an exhausting struggle to finish world number one at the end of 1998 for a record sixth year, Sampras in the early part of 1999 looked vulnerable for the first time.

Not until he won the Stella Artois title – his first for eight months – two weeks before Wimbledon did the old sparkle at least show signs of returning. It was enough to make one of the finest grass-court players of all time the favourite once again, although not with the same obvious conviction as in most recent years.

Unusually for an Australian, Pat Rafter has always insisted that he does not seriously rate his chances at Wimbledon because he does not move well on grass. That probably explains why in six previous visits he had never gone further than the fourth round.

Yet the seeding committee, clearly sharing the view held by many that once he conquers what seems to be more of a psychological than a practical barrier he will pose a considerable threat, decided he was worth being placed second in terms of his achievement potential.

He is, after all, a natural serve-volleyer, who can also rally from the baseline. No doubt his successive victories in 1997 and 1998 at the US Open also added to the faith they held in him, and he wound up his preparations impressively enough by winning the Rosmalen title on grass on the eve of Wimbledon.

yevgeny KAFELNIKOV

andre AGASSI

3

Yevgeny Kafelnikov (Russia)
Age: 25
Born: Sochi
World ranking: 3

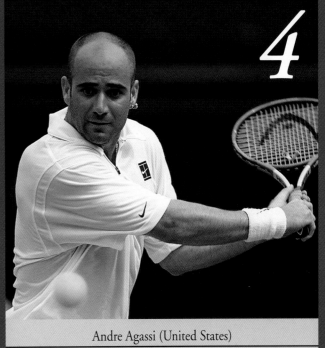

4

Andre Agassi (United States)
Age: 29
Born: Las Vegas, Nevada
World ranking: 4

When he last played in Britain at the Guardian Direct tournament in February, Yevgeny Kafelnikov needed to win only one more match to take over at the top of the world rankings. He missed that opportunity and, although he briefly became the first Russian to reach number one in May, threw away several chances of solidifying his achievement.

In a year when few among the top ten demonstrated the consistency expected of them, thanks to below-par performances rather than always the outstanding form of those who beat them, he went through a stage when he lost his opening match in seven out of eight tournaments.

As a more than competent server, whose outstanding record in doubles is also testimony to his ability at the net and overhead, Kafelnikov's record in never advancing beyond the fourth round at Wimbledon suggested lack of confidence and concentration rather than lack of skill.

Seven years had passed since this swashbuckling American with the charm and ability to have crowds eating out of his hand had won Wimbledon – his first Grand Slam title.

Two weeks before The Championships, this gifted performer whom many had written off in terms of further significant success had won the French Open and become only the fifth man in the history of lawn tennis to have his name on the honours board of all four of the Slams.

Not only that, but in the final he had recovered from being comprehensively outplayed in the first two sets by Andrei Medvedev. The transformation not just in that match but, more particularly, in Agassi's level of self-belief had clearly whetted his appetite for more. Wimbledon, the biggest tennis stage in the world, awaited the game's most popular showman. He gave every indication that he was prepared for the challenge.

richard KRAJICEK

tim HENMAN

5

Richard Krajicek (Holland)

Age: 27

Born: Rotterdam

World ranking: 5

6

Tim Henman (Great Britain)

Age: 24

Born: Oxford

World ranking: 6

The 6ft 5in Dutch player, who came through unexpectedly to win Wimbledon in 1996, had been high on the list of serious challengers for the title again since his successes in winning at Battersea in February, where he beat Greg Rusedski in the final, and then at the Lipton Championships.

He went on record then as admitting he was already 'looking ahead to London in the summer'. On his day the Krajicek serve can be as lethal as any, as he had demonstrated on the Centre Court a year earlier when, although beaten by Goran Ivanisevic in the semi-finals, he struck 42 aces, 23 of them in a pulsating fifth set.

Too often in the past his progress towards the top had been checked by recurring knee problems which ultimately had made it necessary for him to spend time at the end of 1997 and 1998 recovering from surgery on both legs but, with injuries hopefully behind him, his hopes of repeating his 1996 triumph were rising.

After becoming the first British player to reach the semi-finals of the men's singles for 25 years in 1998, there was even greater pressure on Tim Henman this year as the belief that he could become the first British champion since Fred Perry in 1936 was heavily fuelled by an equally enthusiastic media.

Henman himself did nothing to dampen such hopes. Happy at the way his all-round game had continued to broaden and mature in the previous 12 months and further encouraged by a reasonable clay-court season, he genuinely believed that he stood at least as good a chance as most of winning the title.

The key, as always, would be how consistently and effectively he served. There was no questioning his commitment, skill, flair or courage. That had been illustrated often enough. It was largely a case now of his eradicating momentary lapses of concentration and taking the chances he knew he could create. It was an exciting, but also a daunting possibility.

mark PHILIPPOUSSIS

todd MARTIN

Mark Philippoussis (Australia)
Age: 22
Born: Melbourne
World ranking: 11

Todd Martin (United States)
Age: 28
Born: Illinois
World ranking: 14

Just before Wimbledon in 1998, Mark Philippoussis was in such despair about his form going into The Championships that, momentarily at least, he thought it might be wiser for him to fly to his home in Miami and take an extended break from lawn tennis.

Apart from loss of form, his strained relationships with other Australian players over his refusal to play in the Davis Cup added to the pressure he was under. But he had second thoughts, succeeded in reaching the last eight – his best to date at The Championships – went on to play in his first Grand Slam final at the US Open and made peace with Tennis Australia by renewing his support of the Davis Cup team.

John Newcombe, the Australian Davis Cup captain, has often said that Philippoussis, whose fastest serve is second only to Greg Rusedski's in the officially timed list, has the potential to be world number one, although that presupposed that other parts of his game, especially his volleys, will become as effective. There were signs of that happening.

If ever a player allowed his racket to do the talking it has surely always been Todd Martin, which in some ways is a pity because when this quiet, but commanding, 6ft 6in right-hander can be persuaded to express his views on a wide range of subjects in public they are usually worthy of attention.

On court Martin had only once fallen out of the top 20 in the previous six years and that was because of shin and elbow injuries, which forced him off the tour for seven months in 1997. An ideal figurehead for the players as President of the ATP Tour Player Council, he was 'definitely one of the dark horses to keep an eye on this time', according to Tim Henman.

A year earlier, when the 1994 runner-up at the Australian Open reached the semi-finals at Wimbledon for the second time in three years, he suffered a calamitous collapse of confidence when leading MaliVai Washington 5–1 in the final set, which he eventually lost 10–8. Yet through dedicated training he had fully restored not only his own confidence, but also that of others in him.

martina HINGIS

steffi GRAF

Martina Hingis (Switzerland)
Age: 18
Born: Kosice, Slovakia
World ranking: 1

Steffi Graf (Germany)
Age: 30
Born: Bruhl, Germany
World ranking: 3

During an outstanding year in 1997 and a sequence of equally formidable performances in the first five months of 1998, Martina Hingis broke one lawn tennis record after another. And although there were times in the months that followed when her zest for the game seemed to slip the way she recovered to win the Chase Championships in December and then the singles and doubles at the Australian Open for an astonishing third time in succession in January this year suggested that the Swiss teenager with such magnificent touch and style was ready for added greatness.

Yet, just when it looked as if she was ready to sweep all before her once more, a touch of arrogance, which all great champions obviously need, but just as importantly have to know when to show, led to her defeat in such traumatic, emotionally damaging circumstances against Steffi Graf at the French Open.

How quickly would she recover? Would what happened in Paris perhaps make her even stronger and more determined to repeat her first Wimbledon triumph in 1997?

It may have been three years since Steffi Graf had won the last of her seven Wimbledon titles, but her confidence going into The Championships was sky-high after the way she had battled back from a set and 5–3 down to win the 22nd Grand Slam title of her career against Hingis in Paris two weeks earlier.

For Graf, whom Chris Evert described as 'a great champion, perhaps the greatest of all time', every match she won after returning from knee surgery, which could easily have ended her career in the summer of 1998, was a bonus. And nowhere over the years had her game flourished so powerfully, confidently and resiliently as at Wimbledon, with which she had enjoyed a love affair since first competing in the singles back in 1984.

Between 1988 and 1996, she earned a match record of 54–2. 'I'm playing now because I want to and because I enjoy it – not because I feel I have anything to prove,' she said and underlined her much more relaxed approach by confirming her mixed doubles entry with John McEnroe.

lindsay DAVENPORT

monica SELES

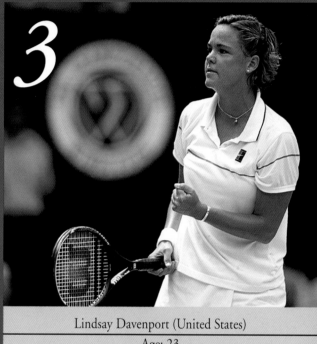

Lindsay Davenport (United States)
Age: 23
Born: California
World ranking: 2

Monica Seles (United States)
Age: 25
Born: Novi Sad, Yugoslavia
World ranking: 4

Lindsay Davenport, least of all, would have questioned the decision to seed Steffi Graf one place above her at Wimbledon even though she was one place higher than the brilliant German in the world rankings.

Davenport readily accepted that in six previous visits to The Championships, although she reached the quarter-finals in 1994 and 1998, she had never fulfilled the expectations of those who felt that her height, reach and heavy-hitting game ought to make her a much greater threat on grass.

One of the past problems for this delightfully engaging Californian had often seemed to be a self-consciousness about her size, which made it more difficult for her to turn it to healthy and exciting advantage. However, after she won the US Open in 1998, there were signs of this beginning to change. She had slimmed down, improved her mobility and started to serve and volley with the consistent confidence of a true champion.

Although the strategy and the shots remained the same, somehow the intensity and the sting had been missing from Monica Seles' relentless pounding game for several months by the time she arrived for Wimbledon '99.

Few would ever begrudge more major titles for the always neat, no-nonsense player with the ability to deliver double-handed winners on both flanks with such power and accuracy, after the way her career was so savagely disrupted in 1993 just when it seemed to be reaching a peak.

At the time of that infamous Hamburg stabbing, Seles had won seven of the eight previous Grand Slam tournaments in which she had played. Since her return, 27 months later, there has been just one more and, although she reached the final of the French Open in 1998 a few weeks after her father and coach died following a long fight against cancer, the sparkle in her eyes – and in her tennis – had never seemed quite the same since.

jana NOVOTNA

venus WILLIAMS

Jana Novotna (Czech Republic)
Age: 30
Born: Brno, Czech Republic
World ranking: 5

Venus Williams (United States)
Age: 19
Born: California
World ranking: 6

It may have taken her 13 years to achieve but, as Jana Novotna said as she looked back on that glorious moment in 1998 when she could at last hold up the Wimbledon trophy in her own right, 'I feel fulfilled.'

What made Novotna's triumph so special was not just the success for a player who had known such heartbreak in two earlier finals, but also the knowledge that the title had gone to a classic grass-court player, one, sadly, of a dying breed.

Novotna's style, more often than not stroking rather than thumping beguiling winners into the space she had created, and her seemingly leisurely stride between points, almost looked out of place in an age of increasingly powerful and frenetic teenage aggression. But her prospects of retaining the title were already beginning to look slim even before the ankle injury that she brought with her from an accident while playing doubles in Paris.

Few players, especially teenagers, have hit groundstrokes with quite so much power as Venus Ebone Starr Williams, who began providing headlines from the day she made her first appearance on the WTA Tour in 1994 and raced to a 6–3, 3–0 lead over Aantxa Sanchez-Vicario.

Williams lost but it was not long before she was winning and, together with her sister, Serena – who was also seeded until she was forced to withdraw from The Championships suffering from influenza – bringing a whole new approach to the style and confident promotion of women's tennis, especially in the United States, where she was a finalist at the US Open in 1997 and a semi-finalist the following year.

Her game is clearly better suited to hard courts than grass, where the low bounces, especially to the backhand, can be more of a problem to someone of her height (6ft 1in), but she was a real threat nevertheless.

arantxa
SANCHEZ-VICARIO

nathalie
TAUZIAT

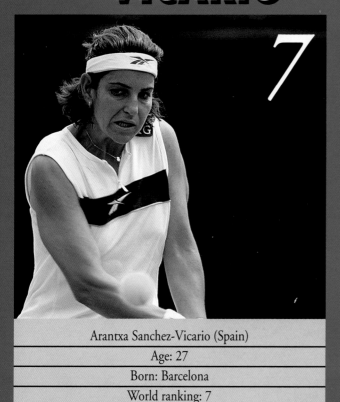

7

Arantxa Sanchez-Vicario (Spain)
Age: 27
Born: Barcelona
World ranking: 7

8

Nathalie Tauziat (France)
Age: 31
Born: Central African Republic
World ranking: 8

Nippy, resilient and fiercely determined: these are three qualities that have always figured prominently in Arantxa Sanchez-Vicario's game. Indeed her ability to retrieve and eventually turn defence into attack has become legendary, enabling her to stay in the top ten of the world rankings since 1989.

Although the Spaniard learned the game on clay, her ability to adapt her style, relying heavily on consistent attrition, is well underlined by a record which shows that in addition to winning the French Open three times – the first in 1989, the most recent in 1998 – she has also been a finalist at the three other Grand Slam tournaments.

Her best performances at Wimbledon came in 1995 and 1996 when, in both years, she was involved in magnificent finals against Steffi Graf, especially the former when she won the first set and pushed the German to 7–5 in the third. Though no longer one of the top challengers, she remains tough to beat.

In some respects life began at 30 for Tauziat who, for the previous 14 years, had often been there or thereabouts in tournaments without making a huge impact, but without suffering too many shock defeats either. In 1998 she not only broke into the top ten for the first time but, at the 43rd attempt, also reached her first Grand Slam final – at Wimbledon.

A measure of her consistency was that earlier this year she won her 500th match on the WTA Tour, becoming the first French player to do so, and joined an exclusive club which by then included only 17 other members.

Her ability to take the ball early and move in to put away volleys had brought her other grass-court successes in Britain in pre-Wimbledon tournaments at Eastbourne in 1995 and Edgbaston two years later, so it was appropriate that the great moment of her career should have been attained at The Championships, but her pre-Wimbledon form this time had not been encouraging.

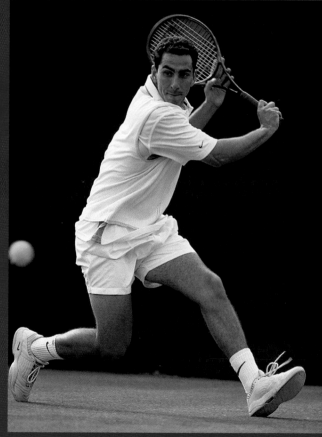

The last Championships of the Millennium could hardly have made a more exhilarating and exciting start. A record opening-day crowd of 36,471 poured into the always colourful and immaculately prepared grounds of the All England Club. The 40 per cent chance of showers, which had been forecast, never materialised as a brisk breeze happily blew the sometimes menacing clouds overhead away from SW19, allowing all but two of the 64 listed matches to be completed. And to cap such pleasures, a little-known British player produced the upset of the day to steal the limelight from the principal star performers, defending champion Pete Sampras and the two leading domestic contenders, Tim Henman and Greg Rusedski.

Out on a packed Court 13, Arvind Parmar, a 21-year-old qualifier from Hertfordshire, made an astonishing recovery from losing the first nine games against Albert Costa to beat the Spaniard, who had spent the three previous years among the world's top 20, 0–6, 7–6, 6–3, 6–3 – a victory that meant Parmar would then be playing Rusedski.

Until this breakthrough, Parmar, a modest 455 in the world rankings, had made little impact since leaving the juniors. However, two weeks earlier the 6ft 3in right-hander had qualified for the Stella Artois Championships at Queen's Club. The confidence of that effort was sustained through the qualifying at Roehampton, where he won three matches to earn the opportunity of what was to be a record £11,000 pay-day. The way he steadied himself after he 'panicked a bit' during what he admitted was a terrible start was superb. He still had to save two set points in the ninth game of the second, as well as break back from a serve down in the third, before he started to take the initiative.

One down, six to go was the dominant thought in Henman's mind after he had edged through his opening match in less than convincing fashion. He suffered another of his all-too-familiar lapses of concentration before finding the author-

ity he needed again in a fourth-set tie-break to beat former world junior champion Arnaud Di Pasquale 6–4, 6–0, 3–6, 7–6 on Court No. l.

All was going swimmingly for Henman as his game took off once he had gained the important first service break to lead 4–3 in the opening set. Two sets were already in the bag and he was serving for 4–2 in the third. Then, as he admitted, 'it went pear-shaped pretty quickly, didn't it?' Two double faults in succession, which cost him his serve, changed the whole complexion of the match to such an extent that Di Pasquale, who had looked the novice he was on grass, especially when it came to digging up Henman's deep groundstrokes into the corners, was playing serve-and-volley tennis in the fourth set.

In the tie-break Henman regained control with a stunning forehand winner down the line. He went on to take it 7–1 in a manner that made the way he had struggled for the previous 45 minutes all the more frustrating.

By contrast Rusedski was in ruthless

Above: A confident enough start to the fortnight by Tim Henman, despite the loss of a set to Frenchman Arnaud Di Pasquale.

Opposite: Arvind Parmar (bottom left) overcame a nervous start to upset the vastly more experienced Spaniard, Albert Costa (bottom right). The surprise result is confirmed on the scoreboard.

form as he brushed aside the 1996 semi-finalist, Australian Jason Stoltenberg, 6–1, 6–4, 6–2 in a mere 79 minutes. Rusedski, who was given a standing ovation as he walked on to Centre Court, fully deserved the acclaim he also received at the end for, other than a double fault on the first point, one could count his total of unforced errors on one hand.

Danny Sapsford's original role at Wimbledon this time was to have been as part of the liaison team escorting players to the media interview room. Instead he became one of those facing the questions following his impressive effort in dismissing the Spaniard, Julian Alonso, 6–2, 6–2, 7–5. In what was to be his farewell as a competitor, before taking up a coaching post with The Lawn Tennis Association, Sapsford served well and also struck plenty of his characteristic backhand winners on Court No. 4, for an impressive straight-sets victory. He had clearly benefited from winning three qualifying matches at Roehampton as he reached the second round for the second time in three years.

Few watching Sampras begin another defence of his title would have predicted how triumphantly it would end. Not once on his first seven service points did he put the ball in play. Then came an ace to settle the butterflies, which even six-times champions can have when they first walk out on Centre Court the following year and he was on his way. Indeed he said he 'could not be happier' after what became his straightforward 6–3, 6–4, 6–4 defeat of Australian left-hander Scott Draper, when one break of serve in each set was enough to keep him in almost total control.

After seven first-round defeats in his previous 11 tournaments, Yevgeny Kafelnikov must have had misgivings about a first-round clash with the big-serving Swede, Magnus Larsson. Such apprehension was justified. Larsson served for the match at 5–4 in the final set, but his serve, which had been so effective, suddenly lost its accuracy and it was a relieved Russian who saw officials waiting

to call them off because of the bad light the moment he had broken back to 5–5. It was the closest shave of the day for any of the seeds in action.

Needless to say, the first day's focus of attention in the ladies' singles was on Anna Kournikova. She faced a daunting first-round test against Barbara Schwartz,

Greg Rusedski (opposite) was quickly into impressively forthright form as he dismissed former semi-finalist Jason Stoltenberg (below) in straight sets.

Yevgeny Kafelnikov (opposite) needed all his resolve to bring Sweden's Magnus Larsson (left) to his knees.

Monica Seles (below) stays focused.

Anna Kournikova (bottom), who prefers sitting sideways to the court, also had to concentrate hard to beat Barbara Schwartz.

Opposite: American Venus Williams launches into action.

Louise Latimer (below) and Karen Cross (bottom right) provided first-round British cheer.

For the first time, spectators, as well as the media, on Centre and No. 1 Courts were able to see for themselves the speed of serves on special display units provided by IBM. The very first official serve on Centre Court was delivered by defending champion Pete Sampras at 127 mph, although before that his opponent, Scott Draper, struck one practice serve with such ferocity that it punched a hole in the side of the equipment.

the Austrian who created such a surprise at the French Open when, as a qualifier, she upset Venus Williams. Kournikova won 7–6, 4–6, 6–2, but having been 1–5 in the second set she knew she would have to attack with far more consistency in future rounds to justify the seeded status she had been granted after Serena Williams withdrew, following the draw, citing influenza.

The change also brought Kournikova to a new slot in the draw and a potential last-16 meeting with Venus, who raced to a 6–1, 4–0 lead against Holland's Miriam Oremans before a combination of wayward ground-strokes from the American and sterner resistance from her opponent contributed to the second set reaching 5–5. 'I think I became over-confident,' said Williams, who delivered one serve at 123 mph, only 4 mph short of her record. 'You have to serve and volley here, but the baseline is just in my blood and I couldn't get it out,' she added, after an Oremans double fault helped her break serve again and round things off at 7–5.

No first-day problems for a beaming Steffi Graf. She breezed past the Slovakian teenager, Ludmila Cervanova, 6–1, 6–4, with impressive flashes of her forehand in over-drive. Monica Seles, the fourth seed, was less convincing but nor was she ever under serious pressure as she beat the Spaniard, Cristina Torrens-Valero, 6–3, 6–1, taking four match points to do so.

Two British ladies went home happy after beating opponents more than 100 places above them in the rankings.

Karen Cross, the Devon player who had been within a point of reaching the last 16 two years earlier, beat the rising American prospect, Lilia Osterloh, 6–1, 6–4, despite trailing 0–3 in the second set, while Louise Latimer progressed 6–4, 6–2 against Anne-Gaelle Sidot of France. Latimer, who impressively imposed her authority once she broke Sidot in the third game, called it her best win and said, 'I knew if I played as well as I had done in Eastbourne [a week earlier] I could do well.'

Disappointment, though, was apparent on the face of Sam Smith, then still the British number one – and the only home player to be accepted on ranking merit straight into the draw – after she suffered a 6–1, 1–6, 6–2 first-round defeat against Ines Gorrochategui, which she knew would send her plunging down the rankings: from 91 to 172. Despite a rousing second set, the Essex girl was well below the form that took her to the last 16 the previous year, and once her Argentinian opponent sensibly began chipping and charging more often at the start of the final set, the initiative was too easily wrested from her.

Previous pages: Spectators enjoyed Andre Agassi's bright start.

Above: Jelena Dokic unleashes one of the powerful forehands that stunned the crowd on No. 1 Court, as well as top seed Martina Hingis, to produce one of the biggest shocks of the year.

Of all the first-round surprises there have been over the years, few have matched the shock impact of the way top-seeded, former champion Martina Hingis was not simply beaten, but out-played and humiliated by the 16-year-old Australian, Jelena Dokic.

Only twice before had a top seed or defending champion lost her opening match in the ladies' singles in modern times. In 1962, when the top seed was automatically given a bye into the sec-ond round, Margaret Court, then Mar-garet Smith, found herself ambushed by Billie Jean King, then still Billie Jean Moffitt. In 1994, Steffi Graf, who had won the title in all of the three previous years, was stunningly beaten on a cold, damp evening, after the weather had de-layed play for several hours, by the American, Lori McNeil.

This, however, was an even more stunning defeat than either of those, even though Hingis had spoken enthusi-astically about the potential of the Yu-goslavian-born Dokic when beating her 6–1, 6–2 at the Australian Open in Jan-uary, because there was almost universal support for the theory that, after her temperamental collapse from a winning position against Graf in the French Open final two weeks earlier, the Swiss 18-year-old would be even more deter-mined to make amends at Wimbledon.

What few knew before the two teenagers walked out on No. 1 Court – Hingis to a mute reception, which sug-gested that the public were not yet ready to forgive, let alone forget, her acknowl-edged misbehaviour at Roland Garros – was that her normally ever-present mother, Melanie Molitor, was back

Left: The strain is etched on Hingis's face as the match runs away from her.

Below: Fiona Edwards, one of Britain's top international umpires, who is also a high flyer in her other career as a flight attendant for a major airline.

home in Switzerland with her partner, Mario Widmer. They had agreed, by common consent, Hingis insisted, to give each other a little more space, at least for the time being, although the timing of the split beggared belief. Hingis admitted that it was the first time she had played a match of significance without the support of her mother nearby – and that it mattered.

One can only guess at the full extent of the impact such an emotional up-heaval had on the match, but Hingis was not overwhelmed only by her opponent's fine winners. For 54 minutes the crowd on Court No. 1 watched in growing dis-belief as Dokic produced an almost con-stant flow of stunning drives. Hingis's failure to get to grips with an ever-wors-ening situation as she was outplayed and outwitted in every aspect of the match

was as surprising as the outcome. Dokic, for whom the former British Davis Cup player, Andrew Richardson, had been brought in to be a hitting partner, swept one amazing groundstroke winner after another. Hingis lost the opening game of the second set on a baseline over-rule by the umpire, Fiona Edwards. Momentar-ily it looked as if she might protest but, perhaps remembering what had hap-pened two weeks earlier in Paris, when she brought the crowd's wrath down upon her, she thought better of it. The rest of the set and indeed the match was largely a virtuoso performance from Dokic, who found the lines too regularly for it to have been pure chance.

It completely overshadowed Jana Novotna's excitement at making the de-fending champion's traditional start to the Centre Court programme on Ladies'

Below: Andre Agassi acknowledges the support and appreciation of the Centre Court crowd.

Opposite: A testing start for defending champion Jana Novotna and her injured ankle.

Day. Not that she minded. While understandably anxious about how well her recently injured ankle would respond, Novotna enjoyed something of a double bonus. First the ankle passed its test perfectly, as she skipped to a 6–2, 6–1 victory over Shi-Ting Wang, which was as comfortable as it sounds. Then, when she returned to the locker room, she learned about the calamity that had befallen Hingis, her principal rival in the top half of the draw.

Novotna was never in trouble from the moment she broke for 3–2 in the opening set against her 73rd-ranked opponent and went on to win in what she said were '47 minutes I will always cherish'.

She was not alone in believing, privately at least, that her prospects had been boosted by the sudden departure of Hingis, who that evening also withdrew from the doubles. It was a decision that left Anna Kournikova, to whom she had turned after deciding that Novotna, with whom she had won the doubles title a year earlier, was 'too old and too slow', without a partner. Mary Pierce, too, had taken note and she was always in control as she hit her expected quota of statuesque winners in a 6–3, 6–2 defeat of the Colombian, Fabiola Zuluaga.

Equally without fuss or bother, Lindsay Davenport took her first steps along what was to become an increasingly memorable path for the American by taking 56 minutes to beat the French player, Alexandra Fusai, 6–0, 6–3, while Jennifer Capriati had emerged triumphant in a stern battle with Anke Huber, which had been the second match halted at 5–5 in a final set by bad light the night before. Both players lost their serve on the resumption, not just once, but twice, before Capriati at last held for 8–7 and then broke the German again to complete her 5–7, 6–3, 9–7 win.

Yevgeny Kafelnikov applied the *coup de grace* against Magnus Larsson, after their overnight delay, much more swiftly. He won the additional two games necessary for him to round off a 6–7, 7–5, 7–6, 4–6, 7–5 victory in just ten more points. The Russian knew only too well, however, that it had been an ominously bumpy ride, whereas Andre Agassi, Patrick Rafter and Richard Krajicek, three who began the fortnight as the most favoured challengers for Pete Sampras's title, made efficient progress. Indeed Agassi, who had not hit a ball in anger since holding the French Open trophy aloft 17 days earlier, slipped into top gear immediately as

he tore the Romanian, Andre Pavel, apart, 6–1, 6–2, 6–3.

Agassi's swiftness made it possible for the crowd to welcome another of their favourites, Goran Ivanisevic, the Croatian he had beaten in the 1992 final, in a bonus match on Centre Court. Ivanisevic's only blemish as he beat Sweden's Mikael Tillstrom, helped by 23 aces in a match switched from an outside court, was one loss of his serve early in the third set.

Rafter's 6–3, 6–2, 6–2 defeat of Italian qualifier Christiano Caratti, coming immediately after Dokic had left the same stage, made it seem like Australia Day on Court No. 1, although the Queenslander knew only too well that tougher hurdles lay ahead. Similarly Krajicek was not fooled by the apparent ease of a 6–2, 6–3, 6–1 win against Norwegian Christian Ruud. 'I played pretty well, but to some extent my opponent let me,' said the Dutchman, who struck 20 aces.

After Monday's domestic delights, there might have been two more. Martin Lee held a match point in the final set before losing 9–7 in the fifth to the Argentinian, Guillermo Canas, while on Court No. 2, where upsets so often seem to occur, Miles Maclagan, the world number 298, who came to British tennis by way of Zimbabwe and Scotland, held three match points against an idol who had won the title three times – Boris Becker. For the first two sets Becker, despite enjoying even more support than his British opponent, could have been forgiven for wondering why he had not stood by his word, after losing his 1997 quarter-final against Sampras on the Centre Court, that it would be his final Wimbledon appearance. He had looked slow and sluggish, and here at 4–5 and two sets to one down it looked as if the six months of effort in getting himself ready for Wimbledon '99 had been in vain. Then over the next six points, three of them match points, he delivered a series of winners, including four monstrous serves, which completely changed the momentum of the match.

Becker went on to win 5–7, 6–7, 6–4, 7–5, 6–2 after three hours 53 minutes. The standing ovation was prolonged and heartfelt, although mixed in with it was sympathy for Maclagan. As Sue Mott wrote in *The Daily Telegraph* the following day, 'We had witnessed the stark divide between a man who cannot forget he is a champion and a man who couldn't believe he was about to beat a champion.'

Opposite: Goran Ivanisevic, still searching for that elusive Wimbledon crown.

Below: Miles Maclagan, the pride of Scotland was cruelly defeated after playing the match of his life against Boris Becker.

After the shock of Martina Hingis's departure the day before, most matches fell in line with expectations on Day Three, although there was a 25-minute spell on Centre Court when the crowd fell ominously silent as they feared that Steffi Graf might also suffer a premature defeat.

Looking decidedly uneasy against the sturdy South African, Mariaan De Swardt, who was happily employing precisely the same volatile and versatile serve-and-volley tactics that had enabled her to upset the German in Brighton three years earlier, Graf found herself trailing 1–5 in the opening set. Then generous help from her suddenly inhibited opponent led to a calming of her nerves.

Graf, who since Hingis's defeat had been even more heavily backed to move within one of Margaret Court's all-time record of 24 Grand Slam singles titles, initially teetered on the brink as she was ruthlessly brushed aside by De Swardt's free hitting. She needed to hold serve in the seventh game, at which stage normal service began to be resumed. Once Graf broke for 3–1 in the second set she was never seriously threatened again, but her relief was evident after she put away a blistering forehand as she served out for a 4–6, 6–3, 6–2 success in 87 minutes. 'I felt like a spectator myself in that first set,' said Graf. 'I had no idea where the balls were going. Had she continued the way she was playing there would have been nothing I could have done. But fortunately I figured out her serve. I guess it was experience which made the difference in the end.'

By contrast with the way Graf had to fight, the other seeds in this half of the draw, notably Monica Seles, Venus Williams and the 1998 runner-up, Nathalie Tauziat, were easing, rather than steaming, ahead, along with 17th seed Anna Kournikova. The Russian teenager, who allowed a big lead to slip away against Tauziat in the Eastbourne semi-finals, again showed a tendency to struggle when closing out a match. Having looked assured of a comfortable pas-sage when breaking twice for a 4–1 second-set lead against the skilful Venezuelan, Maria Alejandra Vento, she allowed her tenacious opponent back into the match and looked grateful in the end when her crunching forehands returned in time for her to win 7–5, 6–4.

Opposite: Anna Kournikova slips over, but sees the funny side.

Below: Monica Seles, as determined as ever in reaching the third round.

Williams did not have her own way either when she followed Kournikova on to the same court against the Ukrainian, Elena Tatarkova, and had to recover from a break down in the second set before going on to win 6–3, 6–4. 'I think I played satisfactorily, but it was not my best tennis,' said the American.

British interest in the ladies' singles was snuffed out when the highly talented Belgian prospect, Kim Clijsters, at 16 years two weeks the youngest singles competitor, thrashed Karen Cross 6–2, 6–0, but a battling Louise Latimer was doing her utmost on Court 4 to stave off defeat by France's Sarah Pitkowski. Three times the Warwickshire player defiantly saved match points, but then a careless forehand ended her hopes and she went out 7–5, 5–7, 6-1.

Among the men, the Union flag continued to fly prominently. Arvind Parmar, the 21-year-old from Hitchin, at least played close enough to his potential to suggest that he was now ready to start seriously improving his modest world ranking of 455, but it was never likely to be enough to deflect Greg Rusedski from his goal. Rusedski hit 17 aces, including one spectacular sequence of six on his way to the tie-break, in a 6–3, 6–4, 7–6 victory.

Parmar was not overawed, but although there was only one break in each of the first two sets and none in the third, it was as much as Rusedski needed because in the first set, which lasted only 22 minutes, Parmar was able to salvage only two points on his opponent's serve. 'Serving like that he'd be a strong favourite for the tournament,' said Parmar. 'He hit serves which you just can't do anything about. The only way is to try and guess which side he's going, but he mixes it up so well that you don't really have any idea which way he's going.'

Danny Sapsford continued to be 'demob happy'. The prospect of giving up the pressures of competitive tennis to become a coach had clearly had a massive relaxing effect on the 30-year-old

from Surrey, enjoying the best Wimbledon of his career without help from a wild card. His ranking of 595 meant he had also had to take part in pre-qualifying for The Championships, so his 6–3, 3–6, 6–4, 6–2 defeat of the Spaniard, Galo Blanco, who never looked happy on the grass, was in reality his eighth win in the tournament. The match itself was overshadowed by what might happen next: Sapsford had earned the right to take on Pete Sampras, who advanced 6–4, 6–2, 6–3 against the Canadian, Sebastian Lareau, but was clearly not happy about losing his serve in the first and third sets.

The likelihood of a third British player reaching the last 32 was held in abeyance overnight. Tim Henman was already leading 6–4, 2–3 on serve against the American, Chris Woodruff, when a match that had not started until just after 7 p.m., owing to the length of the two preceding matches, was stopped by

Opposite, top: Belgium's Kim Clijsters, just 16, the youngest competitor in the ladies' singles, outplayed Karen Cross.

Opposite, bottom: The renewed hopes of former semi-finalist Jennifer Capriati (shown here) were ended by Dutch qualifier Seda Noorlander.

Below: Danny Sapsford earned himself a showpiece third-round match against Pete Sampras by defeating Galo Blanco.

Greg Rusedski progressed to the third round at the expense of another British player, Arvind Parmar.

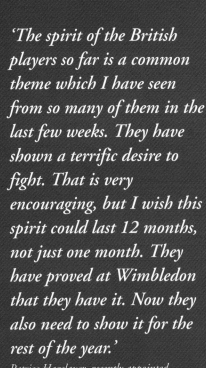

'The spirit of the British players so far is a common theme which I have seen from so many of them in the last few weeks. They have shown a terrific desire to fight. That is very encouraging, but I wish this spirit could last 12 months, not just one month. They have proved at Wimbledon that they have it. Now they also need to show it for the rest of the year.'

Patrice Hagelauer, recently appointed performance director for the LTA.

mutual agreement because of the fast-fading light.

For most of the afternoon the Centre Court had been occupied by Jim Courier and Carlos Moya. Few observers, British Davis Cup supporters least of all, needed reminding how much the feisty American loves a fight, but he demonstrated it yet again when a disputed line-call seemed to inspire him to an even more aggressive level to oust the 12th-seeded Spaniard, 6–3, 3–6, 7–6, 3–6, 6–2 after three hours two minutes.

It was a gripping contest from the start, with Moya possessing a welcome willingness for a Spaniard to serve and volley with real urgency and conviction after first and second serves, especially when he romped away with the third-set tie-break 7–1. The turning point came when Moya, who has never played better on grass, was serving at 1–2, 30–15. Courier remained defiantly unimpressed when French umpire Bruno Rebeuh ruled, quite correctly, that his return, which had landed on the baseline, could not count because it had been just outside the sideline.

His lashed service return one point later showed exactly how he felt. Although Moya held for 2–2, two games later Courier produced two scorching double-handed, backhand cross-court returns to break to 15 and there was no stopping him after that. 'I had to go into a different gear at the end because of the way he was volleying,' said Courier. 'I don't know if I can return much better than that and he just kept coming up with great volleys all the time.'

Felix Mantilla, still vulnerable on grass, became the second Spanish seed to lose on the day when he went down 6–2, 6–4, 6–7, 6–2 to the American, Paul Goldstein, while third seed Yevgeny Kafelnikov again made surprisingly heavy weather of things, losing the opening set to Thailand's 254-ranked Paradorn Srichaphan, before emerging a 6–7, 6–4, 7–6, 6–4 winner on his fourth match point.

The most consistently ferocious serv-ing of the day came from Mark Philip-poussis, who hit an astonishing 38 aces on his way to eventually breaking the skilful and determined resistance of his Australian compatriot, Mark Wood-forde, 6–7, 7–6, 7–6, 6–4. Early on, Philippoussis had been ominously erratic, but ultimately the constant barrage of his serves held sway, even though Woodforde stayed resilient to the end and had two chances to break back in what proved to be the final game.

Carlos Moya (opposite) and Jim Courier (below) cleverly mixed skill with power in a magnificent contest on Centre Court.

WIMBLEDON

day **4**

THURSDAY 24 JUNE

Previous pages: LLeyton Hewitt.

Chris Woodruff (below) was hardly allowed a look-in by Tim Henman (opposite).

After the one hour 13 minutes Tim Henman and Chris Woodruff spent on court the night before, it took Henman almost exactly the same additional time to complete a 6–4, 6–3, 7–6 victory that was encouragingly positive rather than spectacular.

The only cause for concern was that once again Henman lost his focus and almost the initiative just when he appeared to be in full flow. After holding his first service game on the restart to love and breaking just as convincingly with a fine backhand to the baseline, he won four games in just 13 minutes to secure the second set. He also took the opening two games of the third before there was a hiccup as he dropped his own serve to 15 on a double fault one game later.

'It was unsettling when he had that break and got back into it, but I stuck with it and it was a good sign for me that in a tight situation I kept my nose in front with some pretty good serving and volleying,' said Henman, who went on to take the tie-break 7–4 when his opponent, offered another chance by an overhit forehand, then wasted it with a double fault.

The feature of the day's play was again the smooth progress made by the leading contenders in the bottom half of the draw, Messrs Rafter, Agassi and Krajicek in particular. Yet even this dynamic trio was overshadowed by Boris Becker as he returned to his beloved Centre Court to beat one of his top German successors, Nicolas Kiefer, who became the third victim among the 16 seeds.

As the school of potential sharks in the top half of the draw continued to bare their teeth, none even began to attract so much attention as Becker. He was welcomed back on to the Centre Court, which two years earlier he had insisted would play no further part in his life, as a returning hero. Then, as he rounded off an impressively emphatic 6–4, 6–2, 6–4 defeat of his overawed fellow countryman, the cheers could not have been louder had he just become champion for a fourth time.

Many spectators were on their feet even before Kiefer's final backhand return on match point fell against the net. The master had powerfully, and often spectacularly, given the pupil a lesson, in terms not just of experience, but also of grass-court tactics and court craft. His serving was fantastic. There were 17

Below: Tommy Haas underlined his fighting spirit by beating Richard Fromberg from two sets down.

aces, including one on each of the break points he had to save and another, just as significantly, at 0–30 when he served for the opening set – that high kicking second serve down the middle. And, having dismissed one new-generation prospect, Becker was eagerly looking forward to being challenged by another, the 35th-ranked Australian teenager, LLeyton Hewitt, whose swashbuckling style and fine pace about the court had been too much

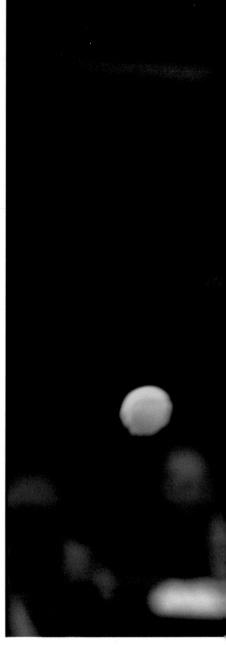

for Karim Alami of Morocco, 6–1, 6–4, 4–6, 6–4.

Agassi gave another formidable impression of his rousing form, especially those blistering returns, as he dismissed the Argentinian, Guillermo Canas, 6–3, 6–4, 6–3, while Todd Martin and Goran Ivanisevic moved another step closer to their expected fourth-round clash when the American beat Jiri Novak 7–6, 6–4, 6–4, and Ivanisevic, who saved six set

points in the opening set, continued to harness his skills without too many set-backs, 7–6, 6–4, 4–6, 6–4, against American-based Australian Sandon Stolle.

Indeed, with Tommy Haas rallying from two sets down to thwart Richard Fromberg and second seed Patrick Rafter beating his doubles partner, Jonas Bjork-man, 6–2, 7–6, 6–7, 6–2 at 8.43 p.m., it meant that seven of the eight seeds in the bottom half were still alive. Not that all

were so confident as two straight-set wins might indicate. Krajicek, the 1996 cham-pion, still did not put his chances of re-peating that triumph as more than 'OK, I guess'. Apart from a couple of consecutive double faults, which led to his losing his serve when he was aiming for a 5–1 lead in the third set, the powerful 6ft 5in right-hander looked well in control from start to finish as he beat the Australian, Todd Woodbridge, a semi-finalist two

Boris Becker provided a lesson for a fellow member of the German Davis Cup team, Nicolas Kiefer.

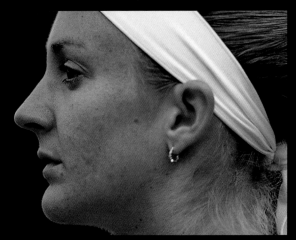

Opposite: Pat Rafter's serve in full flow.

Above: Mary Pierce.

Top: Andre Agassi towels off.

Top right: A few moments to relax for Olga Barabanshikova.

Right: Tony Roche, the Australian Davis Cup coach, had a busy day keeping an eye on Sandon Stolle against Goran Ivanisevic and also Mark Philippoussis, pictured on the following pages.

The often underrated Lisa Raymond was too sharp, especially around the net, for former finalist Arantxa Sanchez-Vicario.

years earlier, 7–5, 6–4, 6–4. Yet, as realistic as ever, but hardly expecting the disaster facing him around the next corner, Krajicek observed, 'I'm progressing, but there are still things I need to improve. I'm not playing my best tennis yet.'

Among the women, just five of the top eight seeds moved into the round of the last 32. The day's most prominent casualty was seventh-seeded Arantxa Sanchez-Vicario, who was uprooted 7–6, 6–1 by the lively American, Lisa Ray-

mond, who looked as comfortable on the grass as the Spaniard is sure-footed on clay. Natasha Zvereva, seeded 16, but with her form still extravagantly wayward at times, also departed – being defeated 6–4, 7–5 by the Russian, Tatiana Panova.

Still no problem for Lindsay Davenport. She brushed aside Karina Habsudova of Slovakia, 6–2, 6–2, in a mere 54 minutes, while Mary Pierce was equally untroubled in her 6–1, 6–3 defeat of the Italian, Rita Grande, even though she was kept on court for 11 minutes longer. Jana Novotna also advanced again in straight sets, 6–3, 6–1, against the Austrian, Sylvia Plischke, although this was by no means a match without concern for the defending champion. There were times when Novotna's lack of mobility and unforced errors made her look anything but convincing.

The loss of two more seeds in this half of the draw inevitably increased the attention on the competitor who had started the damage in the first place, Jelena Dokic. Perhaps not surprisingly in the circumstances, the 16-year-old Australian immigrant from Yugoslavia had infinitely more trouble in overcoming the Slovakian, Katarina Studenikova, than she had in packing Martina Hingis back home so peremptorily in the first round. This time, although there were plenty of winners again, especially as she romped away with the first set to love in 23 minutes, by which time she had won 16 straight games in the singles event, thereafter the unforced errors were almost as numerous. Indeed it was not until she was 2–4 in the third set that Dokic provided evidence of the steel that supports the skill, and she went on to complete a 6–0, 4–6, 8–6 victory.

'It was a little scary today,' she admitted. 'I dropped my game and also my concentration a little. Now I have to keep my feet on the ground and it's hard to do that with all the attention and the press and everything. More people talk to me and everybody knows me. And there's a little more respect.'

Above: Lindsay Davenport powers her way on.

Right: Jelena Dokic found it tougher a second time, squeezing through 8–6 in the third against Katarina Studenikova.

At match point down in a first-round ladies' doubles match, Britain's Jo Ward, partnering Karen Cross, followed Martina Hingis's example at the French Open and tried an underarm serve. It landed in the net, much to the amusement of Nathalie Tauziat, who then dealt summarily with the second effort as she and fellow French player Alexandra Fusai completed a 7–5, 3–6, 6–0 victory.

WIMBLEDON

day 5

FRIDAY 25 JUNE

The secret to winning Wimbledon, many champions have declared over the years, is to play well enough in each match to sustain confidence into the second week, but not to peak too soon. On that basis, Tim Henman and Greg Rusedski had every reason to be as happy as the 13,000 spectators who stood cheering them to the Centre Court rafters as both kept their hopes alive. What attracted rather less attention was that Pete Sampras, without needing to lift his game for sustained periods in bringing Danny Sapsford's career to an end, was doing exactly the same.

Needless to say, most of the domestic media attention was on Henman and

Rusedski. First Henman beat Frenchman Sebastien Grosjean 6–1, 6–7, 6–2. Then, with the light starting to fade, Rusedski completed a 6–3, 6–4, 7–5 defeat of Sweden's Magnus Norman, during which he hit 21 aces, at 8.50 p.m.

For three of the four sets, Henman was on top of his game, serving splendidly, returning aggressively and putting away most of his volleys with a crisp authority that made sure that not even such a quick-moving opponent and talented counter-puncher as Grosjean could send them back. Yet the British player's failure to win in three sets, after he played a poor service game and was broken at 5–4 in the second set, underlined an all-too-familiar problem still needing to be addressed.

There was no lack of incident, action or excitement in the two-hour-47-minute match, but once Henman had broken for 2–1 in the fourth set with a fantastic lob – a tactic Grosjean had successfully employed earlier – the British number one was in full cry and his long-

Below: Noisy, colourful support for Tim Henman (opposite) against Sebastien Grosjean.

term prospects for the fortnight were certainly not harmed when third-seeded Yevgeny Kafelnikov, his potential quarter-final rival, was forced to withdraw at one set all and after one game of the third set with a leg injury against Frenchman Cedric Pioline.

Once Rusedski had saved two break points in the fifth game of his match against Norman, he went on his merry way, swinging into serves and putting away volleys with gusto, although, as with Henman, there was a lack of consistency that might have been punished by a more experienced grass-court player. Serving for the second set, Rusedski had to save two break points before taking it with a winning serve to the backhand and he had to rescue another break point while serving for the match.

Some observers were cynical about the way Sapsford threw his racket into the crowd, where, incidentally, there were plenty fighting to collect it, after the playing career of a competitor ranked only 595 in the world had ended with his 6–3, 6–4, 7–5 defeat by the number one player in the world. True, Sampras, with just one service break in each set, did no more than was necessary, but if you believe the Olympic ethos that it is not so much the winning as the taking part that matters, then Sapsford deserved his final, brief place in the sun. The way he returned one typical Sampras 'slam dunk' as a winner – the return catching the American off guard at his feet – will worthily live in the memory of the diminutive 30-year-old from Surrey, who never stopped trying to make an impact in the game and at least never gave less than 100 per cent every time he walked on any court.

Jim Courier, who would be Henman's

Opposite: Cedric Pioline waits patiently as Yevgeny Kafelnikov receives treatment for a leg injury. However, the latter (below) was forced to tell the umpire was retiring.

next opponent, had to save two match points before overcoming a devastated Dutchman, Sjeng Schalken, 7–6, 3–6, 3–6, 7–5, 13–11, in four hours 27 minutes on Court 3, making it, at least for a few days, the second-longest timed singles match in Wimbledon history. Victory was achieved by the rugged American at a price, for he later left the All England Club on a stretcher chair and took himself to a nearby hospital to be put on an intravenous drip. He had claimed, wrongly, Club officials were quick to stress, that such medical facilities were not available on site. Dr Peter Tudor-Miles, the Club physician, had decided that Courier's condition was not serious enough to need artificial help.

The defining moments for Courier against the slightly higher ranked Schalken came in the fourth set, when he saved one match point at 4–5, and in the fifth when he saved another at 5–6. In all he served to stay in the match seven times against an obdurate opponent, who frequently out-retrieved him, and must have felt he was on the verge of arguably the finest win of his career. On that first match point Courier produced a brilliant, ripping forehand to keep himself in the game. He went on to break one game later and take the set. At 5–6 in the fifth it was a misplaced volley from Schalken that gave Courier his second stay of execution.

By his standards Courier, doubtless also feeling some strain from another five-setter two days earlier and suffering from a head cold, did not play well and he did not help matters by allowing himself to be broken when he served 9–8 ahead in a final set, which ultimately took 97 minutes to reach a conclusion. The next two games also went against the serve to 10–10, but at 11–11 Courier broke again and this time decided it was time for the nonsense to stop. He served out for a place in the fourth round to love.

Other seeds to advance in the same half of the draw were Karol Kucera, taken to four sets by Daniel Vacek, and

Mark Philippoussis, who won in straight sets against the Spaniard, Francisco Clavet, 7–5, 6–4, 6–4, and then spoke about his growing aspirations for the second week. 'Winning Wimbledon is something I've always dreamed of since I was a kid. It seems so much more prestigious than all the other tournaments,' he said.

The singles excitement of the day was

Jim Courier (opposite) and Sjeng Schalken (below) fought out the second-longest timed singles match at The Championships before the American moved into the fourth round.

Monica Seles (below) was outgunned by
Mirjana Lucic (opposite).

Ines Gorrochategui (below) needed treatment after a fall and ultimately had to retire from her hard-hitting encounter with Anna Kournikova (opposite).

by no means confined to the men. In the ladies' singles, Monica Seles, who more than once has said that she will never regard herself as an all-time great unless she wins Wimbledon, was beaten 7–6, 7–6 by Mirjana Lucic. The Croatian teenager, living in Florida, quite simply, but often spectacularly, ousted the fourth seed in a pulsating, relentlessly aggressive encounter by beating her at her own game. The quality of winners from both players was consistently high, but the longer each set lasted, the more one felt that Lucic would prevail in the tie-breaks, which she did, 7–4 on both occasions.

Amanda Coetzer, the 12th seed, was also sent packing. Trading shots from the baseline with almost outrageous aplomb, Belgium's Kim Clijsters, who had only just been ranked high enough to earn a place in the qualifying, earned the right to tackle seven-times champion Steffi Graf with a 6–2, 6–4. victory. For her part Graf took time to settle into her contest with the American, Corina Morariu. The first 11 points went against serve, but the second seed then strode on, taking 11 of the last 13 points to win 6–1, 6–3, leaving her opponent to concentrate on helping Lindsay Davenport in the doubles.

It was a measure of the ease with which Venus Williams had moved into the last 16 with a 6–1, 6–1 victory over 36th-ranked French player Sylvia Pitkowski that the journalists seemed to be more interested in her thoughts on London and various other facets of life on the circuit than in her game. Certainly her third-round match had created little excitement, but that appeared likely to change. Her next test would come from Anna Kournikova, the photographers' dream girl, whose match against Ines Gorrochategui was already taking a topsy-turvy passage before a heavy fall early in the second set forced the Argentinian player to quit when trailing 7–5, 3–1, 15–0.

By now the doubles events were well under way, although none created more attention than when John McEnroe, 40, veteran of three singles and five men's doubles titles at The Championships, walked on to Court No. 1 at 7 p.m. with his new mixed doubles partner, Graf. It was the confirmation of a plot the two had originally talked about many months earlier and there was a standing ovation from a stadium full to overflowing, ready for and expecting some fun. The fans were not disappointed, and while it may not always have been appreciated by Jeff Coetzee of South Africa and a clearly nervous Eva Melicharova of the Czech Republic, the crowd loved every moment. McEnroe set the tone, first by responding to the hero-worship reception by encouraging the fans to make even more noise and then by throwing down his racket in mock disgust as Graf, often finding it hard not to laugh, failed to get her first return of serve back into play. But was it really the right time and the right place?

WIMBLEDON

day6

SATURDAY 26 JUNE

Lorenzo Manta salutes the large contingent of Swiss supporters who hailed the big-serving qualifier's surprise defeat of fifth-seeded Richard Krajicek.

Once again it was Court No. 2 that provided not just the most significant upset on Day Six, but the biggest shock so far in the men's singles. The tall, unheralded Lorenzo Manta from Switzerland, a 24-year-old at last free from a succession of injuries that at least partly explained his lowly world ranking of 196, chose this occasion to serve as he had probably never served before to take full advantage of another decidedly uninspired effort from former champion Richard Krajicek, whom he beat 6–3, 7–6, 4–6, 4–6, 6–4.

At the end of 1998, although he had replaced the retired Jakob Hlasek as doubles partner to Marc Rosset in the Swiss Davis Cup team, Manta had renewed shoulder and arm injuries that made him question the point in struggling on. Then there were problems with blood circulation to the tips of his fingers, which meant that at times he could not even hold the racket properly. All such nightmare memories were now cast aside though, and a player who had not dropped his serve in the qualifying continued in that vein against the fifth seed.

Krajicek was clearly taken by surprise by an opponent who more than matched his 23 aces and hit even more stunning winners down the line. Yet most thought that the Dutchman would claw his way out of trouble when, having struggled back from two sets down, he broke back from 1–4 in the fifth to draw level at 4–4, even though he had to save four more break points in that titanic eighth game, three of them with thunderous aces. Manta, however, refused to quit. He produced three more stunning returns to break for 5–4, and although Krajicek saved the first match point against him with an ace, his free-wheeling rival just hit out even more fiercely on the next with a winning backhand return.

A second qualifier and a third un-seeded player also made it into the fourth round. The other qualifier was Wayne Arthurs, at 28 an even more sea-soned journeyman in lower-grade competitions than Manta, whose serve was also the key to his success as he upset the 14th-seeded German, Tommy Haas, in three tie-breaks. The extra unseeded survivor to the fourth round was, of course, the imdomitable Boris Becker, who bobbed and bounced around the Centre Court like a veritable Peter Pan to beat the brilliant Australian 18-year-old, LLeyton Hewitt, 6–1, 6–4, 7–6.

Many had thought that Hewitt's volatile enthusiasm, together with his powerful counter-hitting from the back of the court and his ability to chase down volleys and drop shots, might be one challenge too many for the German. How wrong they were, although the

Boris Becker was again able to roll back the years and produce a vintage display to dismiss Australian teenage prodigy LLeyton Hewitt.

As Pat Rafter stretches to make a return
the IBM display board shows the speed
of Thomas Enqvist's serve, 122 mph.

Below: Pete Sampras was always in charge as Danny Sapsford's playing career came to an end.

Opposite: Andre Agassi unwittingly markets the official Wimbledon towel.

score provided a totally false indication of how close and probably decisive was the first set. Hoping to catch Becker cold, Hewitt, who won the toss, chose to receive. It nearly worked. The first game lasted seven minutes but, having survived, Becker had already seen enough to know that risk-taking on second serves would be imperative after the way Hewitt had been despatching anything less than a perfect volley.

Although Becker broke twice in the opening set, Hewitt, who seemed to be overawed by the occasion, had double the number of break points (four) without taking any of them and that statistic told the story. Not until the third set, when he at last broke Becker's serve during a spell in which he held 12 consecutive points, did Hewitt threaten seriously, but after escaping two set points in the penultimate game with brutal serves in excess of 100 mph, the former champion took the tie-break 7–5.

Next up for Becker would be second seed Patrick Rafter, who once more demonstrated his growing confidence on the surface by moving into overdrive to beat Sweden's Thomas Enqvist 7–6, 6–2, 6–2 in a late-evening match, which nearly did not finish because of a sharp shower. Rafter was in charge not only at and around the net, but also from the baseline and would have won more comfortably, before the rain, but for Enqvist's bold resistance in the first set. The Swede, who had upset the Australian in front of his own followers in Melbourne in the year's first Grand Slam tournament in January, not only retrieved Rafter's early break of serve with three stunning returns, but also saved four set points in the 7–5 tie-break.

Meanwhile Andre Agassi's tennis fluctuated, as it so often can, between being awesome and clumsy as he took longer and needed more energy than predicted to overcome the under rated Spaniard, Alberto Martin, 6–2, 6–0, 2–6, 6–3. Overwhelmed for two sets, Martin varied his approach with considerable success to dictate the third, and had he accepted his chance of a break point at 3–3 in the fourth set, it would have been fascinating to see if the American would once again have felt like bowing and blowing kisses to all corners of the court.

With no other seed between him and a place in the quarter-finals, it all seemed to be working out pleasingly for Agassi. And after his mainly wretched months

Above: Maria Antonia Sanchez Lorenzo was unable to sustain a 4–1 first-set lead against Jana Novotna.

leading into Wimbledon, Goran Ivanisevic, the 1998 runner-up, was also all smiles after he had dismissed Holland's Paul Haarhuis 7–6, 6–4, 7–6. Haarhuis, who had a 7–4 advantage from their previous 11 meetings, led 4–1 and 5–2 in the third set and held two set points when serving at 5–4, but Ivanisevic broke back, held his own next service game from 15–40 with four winners, including a second serve ace, and went on to clinch the second tie-break of the match 7–3. That meant he would be facing Todd Martin, who was still not looking the threatsome, including Tim Henman, had expected him to be. He had to recover from a set down to beat Germany's Jens Knippschild 6–7, 6–1, 7–6, 7–5.

Most of the action in the ladies' singles was overshadowed by an outburst from Samantha Stevenson, an American journalist whose teenage daughter, Alexandra, had come through as a qualifier to reach the fourth round with a handsome 6–3, 6–3 defeat of 11th-seeded French player Julie Halard-Decugis. Mrs Stevenson's allegations that racism and cattiness had become rife on the WTA Tour, fiercely denied by Tour officials, were to some extent counter-productive because they took away newspaper space and radio time that her daughter would otherwise have filled by the impressive style of her play.

In days when so many on the WTA Tour sport dou-ble-fisted backhands and seem reluctant to leave the baseline voluntarily, Stevenson's single backhand, fierce, flat forehands and impressive serve offered a refreshing throwback to earlier days. Jelena Dokic also cleared another hurdle, although the stress was beginning to tell as she just scraped out a 6–7, 6–3, 6–4 victory over Luxembourg's only top-flight player, Anne Kremer, in a match riddled with errors.

At the other end of the age scale, Jana Novotna, determined to keep the serve-and-volley flag flying at least until someone else, such as Lindsay Davenport, would be ready to take it over from her, trailed 1–4 in the first set before recovering, none too convincingly, to beat the other Sanchez from Spain (Maria Antonia Sanchez Lorenzo) 6–4, 6–3, while Davenport continued her jolly, sufficiently efficient progress 6–3, 6–2 over the Italian, Laura Golarsa.

Right: Anne Kremer, Luxembourg's sole flag carrier, won a set, but became the third victim of Jelena Dokic (opposite).

Opposite: Tim Henman celebrated taking a two-sets-to-one lead against Jim Courier before the rain forced an overnight delay, but in no way dampened the spirits of spectators.

After a first week of almost uninterrupted play, the weather dealt players, spectators and organisers an unfriendly hand on Day Seven, allowing only five of the 16 scheduled men's and ladies' singles matches to be completed. What made it doubly galling was that it had all the hallmarks of being one of the most memorable days in recent years. No fewer than five present or past singles champions were listed to play. It was not to be.

Not only did Tim Henman and Jim Courier have to run for cover just as they had completed their permitted five minutes' warm-up, but their much-vaunted fourth-round clash was later disrupted for 72 minutes in the fourth game and then postponed overnight after two hours 41 minutes, with the British number one tantalisingly just two games away from victory.

Among those left kicking their heels, unable even to get on court, were Greg Rusedski, waiting to face Mark Philippoussis and Boris Becker, a heart-throb from the '80s, due to face Pat Rafter, who holds a similar status in the '90s. Above all, it delayed what promised to be the most compelling ladies' clash, Anna Kournikova v. Venus Williams.

On a day when home pride and expectations somewhat overshadowed the latest remarkable performance from Jelena Dokic as the 16-year-old added the regal Mary Pierce to her lengthening list of conquests, Henman, who had made a shaky start, especially after opening the match with a double fault and losing the game to 15, was the one most often dictating the progress when they had to call a halt.

Certainly it was Courier who appeared most grateful to see the rain start falling again when he was trailing 4–6, 7–5, 7–5, and 4–3 on serve in the fourth set. Few needed reminding about the antecedents which made this such a competitive contest. Only three months earlier, in Birmingham, Courier had first beaten Henman 7–5 in the fifth and then Greg Rusedski 8–6 in the fifth to become the hero of an epic 3–2 Davis Cup victory for the United States over Britain. The mood for revenge was in the air.

Apart from that worrying initial break, there was no time for much to happen in part one, which lasted a few seconds less than 12 minutes. In the remaining two and a half hours that formed part two, the action, like the determination, was intense, with both players holding key chances that either slipped away or were snatched back. Indeed four times after Courier reached break point, Henman's response was to hit aces.

The closing stages of the third set and the way matters were unfolding in the fourth underlined the pressure on both players and the narrow dividing line between winning and losing points on so many occasions. Both men took risks. They had to. The longer the match lasted, the more it appeared that Henman was reaping a higher dividend for such boldness and, having saved two break points, one with an ace, the other with a service winner, at 5–5 in the third set, it was his determination to go in behind his serve at all costs in the next game to ambush Courier from the net that made the difference.

For a while even Courier's broad shoulders dropped, but when he came up with a brilliantly deployed, high kicking serve to save a break point in the

Below: Gustavo Kuerten, a first-round loser on his two previous Wimbledon visits, made sure there was no further giant-killing from Lorenzo Manta, as the Brazilian exceeded his 11th seeding by reaching the last eight, to the delight of his fans (opposite, below left).

sixth game of the fourth set and then forced Henman to strike his tenth ace to deny him a break point in the seventh, everyone knew that the American's instinct for survival, when they departed to sleep on it overnight, was not necessarily extinguished.

In the only two men's singles matches that were decided, Wayne Arthurs and Lorenzo Manta, two of the least likely qualifiers in recent years, were quickly brought back down to earth after the euphoria they rightly felt over the week-

end after beating the seeded Tommy Haas and Richard Krajicek respectively.

Arthurs, 28, an Australian who had moved to live in Watford, England, just over a year earlier, briefly set pulses racing again on Court No. 1 when he recovered from a mini-break down to take a tie-break first set from Andre Agassi. In the end, though, the left-handed heavy server, who had only once before won his way through qualifying at any Grand Slam event in 19 attempts over ten years, was well beaten 6–7, 7–6, 6–1, 6–4.

It was mainly a case of Agassi taking time to assess the threats within Arthurs' leftie serve-and-volley game and then moving through in relative comfort. The match started to turn in the American's favour when, having escaped from 15–40 at 5–5 in the second set, he took another tie-break 7–5 and was able to go on the offensive in a much more free-wheeling manner.

The beginning of the end came in the third game of the third set when Agassi's severe double-fisted returns succeeded where no one else had done in 19 sets and 111 games in three qualifying and six main-draw matches by breaking Arthurs' serve. Arthurs, who had been smelling the roses for longer than he could have imagined, said, 'Those two break points at 5–5 in the second set were my big chance. Against these guys you don't get many chances, so you have to take them.'

Manta found that, with the powder in his serve too often as damp as the weather, he did not have sufficient firepower in his game to worry the fast-improving Brazilian, Gustavo Kuerten, often enough. Nerves did not help. Having recovered from a disastrous start, in which he did not win a point until he was trailing 0–3, he served for the first set at 5–3, but double-faulted and handed back the initiative. Kuerten, despite a lapse of his own when he was poised to win in straight sets, triumphed 7–5, 6–4, 5–7, 6–3 and could then contemplate his plan of action in the quarter-finals against Agassi.

Left: Andre Agassi plays a shot through the legs, which always earns a cheer, on his way to victory against Australian qualifier Wayne Arthurs (below).

Below: Barbara Schett, the Austrian who gave Lindsay Davenport (opposite) her toughest match on the way to the final.

Dokic, one of six teenagers in the last 16 of the ladies' singles, also lost her first three games on Court No. 2 against Pierce before settling but, unlike Manta, once she found a winning way she stayed firmly in charge. The 16-year-old's papa, Damir, sat proudly, but seemingly impassive, any emotions hidden behind the customary dark glasses, as Jelena, despite being given an object lesson in dropshots early on, launched her comeback from 1–4 by spreading her considerable groundstroke talents to all areas of the court. Pierce, not for the first time, crumbled with a lack of resistance that

made one wonder why there has been so much fuss over the body-building supplement, Creatine, she had been taking quite legally. Indeed Pierce's challenge faded to such an extent that it was difficult to decide just how well Dokic, considerably below the heights she attained in beating Martina Hingis, was playing.

One player who had no complaint when the rain interrupted her match was the 6ft 2in American, Lindsay Davenport, whose progress as third seed had passed by almost unnoticed, as she reached the last 16 for the loss of only 12 games in six sets. The world number two was in danger of losing a set for the first time as 14th-seeded Austrian Barbara Schett prepared to serve at 5–3 in the opening set when, after 50 minutes, the rain provided her with the time to reassess and regroup her ideas, with the help of coach Robert Van't Hof. Two and a half hours later when play resumed, Davenport's renewed urgency in her returns enabled her to break back, although the mini-crisis was not over. She still had to save three set points in her next service game and three more in the tie-break before taking her first real chance to change the course of a tight contest.

Meanwhile her next opponent, Jana Novotna, was continuing to make contented, if far from impressive, progress with a 6–3, 7–5 defeat of the French player, Nathalie Dechy. Novotna, still concerned enough about the ankle she injured badly in Paris to have it packed in ice after every match, admitted that her fitness and therefore her form were still below the level she wanted them to be.

Two other fourth-round matches were on court, but unfinished, although Steffi Graf would probably have been safely home had she not been taken to three deuces by Belgian 16-year-old Kim Clijsters when serving for a 5–2 lead in the second set after winning the first 6–2. Mirjana Lucic, the Croatian who had upset Monica Seles, was also 5–5 against Thailand's formidable Tamarine Tanasugarn when the rain sent 36,884 fans home early.

Above: The spectators patiently waited all day for the resumption of Tim Henman's match against Jim Courier but, although Jana Novotna (right) spotted a brief glimpse of blue sky at one stage, the skies just as quickly darkened again.

For more than six hours, the regular updates from the London Weather Centre sustained hopes that some play would eventually be possible. Yet, although it was reported to be fine as little as ten miles away, the rain hardly stopped for more than a few minutes over the grounds of the All England Club, and at 6.40 p.m. came the announcement that play had been abandoned and the full ticket-refund arrangements would apply.

It was as disappointing for the players waiting to compete, whether in singles, doubles or any of the ancillary competitions, as it was for the 29,870 who were in the grounds, especially those who had queued overnight. But, as Ronald Atkin wrote in the Wimbledon programme the next day, the Dunkirk spirit was as strong as ever. Referring to the frustration endured by all concerned on Day Eight, he wrote, 'The champagne lawn was, as ever, crowded. The only difference being that the Pimm's and bubbly were being consumed under umbrellas as water trickled on to trousers and tights.'

The one problem that a grass-court tournament can never escape is rain. And while, in the absence of other issues to write about or discuss, the old chestnut about having a roof over the Centre Court re-emerged in some parts of the media, Tim Henman's coach, David Felgate, spoke for the vast majority when he said, 'I don't think an indoor grass court will really work and in any case I'm a traditionalist. I like it the way it is.'

In other words, one of the reasons why Wimbledon is so special is because it is played on grass, the surface for which lawn tennis was originally devised. And to play some matches under the cover of a roof, while others were left in the backlog, would be unfair to those players and spectators unable to benefit.

Henman, of course, was one of the players left kicking their heels in locker rooms, whiling away the time by turning to backgammon or some other similar activity, or by watching reruns of great Wimbledon matches from the past.

Only once was it possible to lower the tents and then remove the covers from Centre and No. 1 Courts. Spectators looked on with growing expectation as they watched groundstaff mow the grass, re-mark the lines and erect the net. Approaching 2.30 p.m. everyone was taking their places. The ball boys and girls and the line umpires had resumed their stations, and Henman and Jim Courier,

ready to resume where they had left off the night before, with the British number one ahead 4–6, 7–5, 7–5, 4–3, 15–30 on the American's serve, were in the initial throes of the warm-up when – calamity – a light drizzle began falling again.

The look of disbelief and then frustration on the faces of both players as they saw referee Alan Mills beckoning them back to the locker room so that the groundstaff could replace the covers told its own story. For the record, it was only the 30th time – and this was the 113th staging of The Championships – that a complete day's play had been washed out ... although naturally such information was little comfort to those, including one lady and her grandson who had travelled specially from Inverness in Scotland for a once-in-a-lifetime visit, who had waited all day in vain for play to begin.

There are always ways to compensate for the disappointment of no play.

Stefan Edberg became the first recipient of the Jean Borotra Sportsmanship Award presented by the Council of International Clubs at a ceremony before the rain wiped out the prospect of any play on the main courts. 'When I played Marc Rosset in 1991,' Edberg, twice winner of the men's singles title, recalled, 'we were supposed to start at 2 p.m. on Monday and we finished on Thursday. I was here from early morning till late evening four days in a row before we completed the match.'

Used Championships Balls

£2.50 per can
(3 Balls)

£1.00 per ball

Next Ball Sale

Tomorrow

	Miss K. SREBOTNIK
	Miss S. PITKOWSKI
	Miss A-G. SIDOT
	Miss L. LATIMER
	Miss R. DRAGOMIR
	Miss P. SUAREZ
	Miss I. GORROCHATEGUI
	Miss S. SMITH
	Miss M.A.VENTO
	Miss E. GAGLIARDI
	Miss B. SCHWARTZ
	Miss A. KOURNIKOVA
	Miss A.J. COETZER
	Miss N.J.PRATT
	Miss C. PAPADAKI
	Miss M. SAEKI
	Miss J. KRUGER
	Miss K. CLIJSTERS
	Miss L. OSTERLOH
	Miss K.M. CROSS
	Miss K-A. GUSE
	Miss J. LEE

Opposite: After such a fine start, Greg Rusedski (top) was unable to prevent Mark Philippoussis (below) from taking charge with his leaping returns, as well as his serves.

Below: Jim Courier kisses the net after getting a lucky touch in his match with Tim Henman.

It's an ill wind, they say. While the weather had ruined Day Eight for spectators, those arriving on Day Nine found themselves tempted by the Order of Play, left, right and centre. When the gates opened at 10.30 a.m., the most popular stampede – which every morning officials do their best to prevent – by those without seats for Centre or No. 1 Court, was towards Court 18 to claim places for the undoubted ladies' singles match of the day between Anna Kournikova and Venus Williams. Understandably, though, uppermost in most people's minds were the two fourth-round men's singles matches featuring the two remaining British players, Tim Henman and Greg Rusedski. Happily the gremlins that had prevented the large screen behind No. 1 Court from being operative the day before had been cleared, for at the height of the drama, as Henman carried on from where he left off against Jim Courier, there was hardly an inch to spare on the grass bank.

During that wasted time 24 hours earlier, Henman's coach, David Felgate,

had suggested that the first two points at the restart would be crucial and set the pattern for the rest of what would become 'a totally different match'. He was right, although not even he could have predicted just how much of an emotional roller-coaster ride on which Henman would take himself and the spectators, as he saved three match points before arriving in the quarter-finals for a fourth consecutive year.

Henman could have made it short and sweet by winning the fourth set. He had a break point for 5–3, but Courier saved it with an ace and thereafter, as Henman said later, 'It could have gone either way.' That a match started on Monday and finished on Wednesday with a washed-out day between ultimately went his way, 4–6, 7–5, 7–5, 6–7, 9–7, was because the British player 'stuck to it and showed a lot of guts and determination to hang in there'.

Courier had two set points when ahead 6–5 before forcing a fifth set in a 7–5 tie-break, during which, as in the rest of the four hours 30 minutes playing

time, which made it second only to Gonzales v. Pasarell in 1969 in recorded Wimbledon history, the initiative constantly changed. 'I'm just relieved and delighted to get through, especially the way I did so,' said the British number one after the standing ovation that greeted the unreturnable backhand drop-shot volley he played on the one match point he needed.

The final set, during which Courier saved two break points at 2–2 and Henman had been first to the net to save one against him to make it 4–4, came to the boil in the most spectacular manner. Serving at 5–5, Courier, who had three times been the victim of the ball thudding against the net and then dropping on the wrong side for him, benefited from one similiar incident just when he needed it most, on a break point. He also saved a second break point when Henman overhit a backhand before holding for 6–5.

In the following game Courier decided it was time to strike. Two stunning returns left Henman match points down at 15–40. On the first the American went for another big forehand service return, but netted. On the second his backhand into the corner went wide. But one point later Henman was match point down again. Once more the crowd fell silent, only for an explosion of sound to greet the 126 mph ace down the centre line that followed. Another ace at 130 mph enabled Henman to hold, so the excitement continued. Then it was Courier's turn to sweat. Three break points had to be saved before he edged ahead 7–6.

Two games later Courier, almost alone it should be stressed, was convinced that Henman's backhand into the backhand corner, which set up the break point that gave the Oxfordshire player the chance to serve for the match, was out. 'I don't like calls affecting the outcome of matches, but they do and it's a fact of professional tennis,' he said later. 'I'm not really upset about it, I'm used to it and anyway I should have finished the

match before then so I wouldn't have had to worry about it.'

So Henman went on to plot how to tackle Frenchman Cedric Pioline, who had also come through in a match interrupted on Monday, in five sets against Karol Kucera. But no longer did Henman have Greg Rusedski around to share at least some of the domestic pressure with him. The left-hander's serve, on which so much of the rest of his game still depends, suddenly lost its way and he was well beaten 2–6, 7–6, 6–3, 6–1 by the man with the second-fastest serve, Mark Philippoussis.

When Rusedski whizzed through the first set in 26 minutes, seemingly able to hit aces and service winners at will, and complementing them with equally impressive backhand returns and even a few delicate drop-shots, the mood on Court No. 1 was almost euphoric. By the end of the second set, however, during which Rusedski had missed three break points before losing it in the 7–4 tie break, anxiety was setting in. Philippoussis, having already saved one break point at 2–3, had clearly drawn inspiration from the way he rescued the second. He chased back to reach the lob and turned, as if on a sixpence, to lash a wonderful forehand cross-court winner.

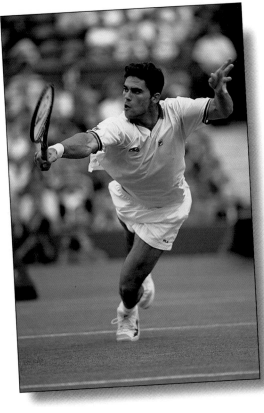

The whole impetus changed and for Rusedski, not helped by a thigh strain that led to treatment from the trainer, it simply went from bad to worse. Twelve double faults and only nine aces were statistics he will not want to recall from what he called 'one of those days'.

'Wimbledon was always very special to me. It made me who I am today and gave me the freedom to do whatever I wanted with my life. It's hard to compare anything with the feeling of walking on to Centre Court, especially if it's for a final. It's an experience which all the players will tell you is one of a kind. This place is like nowhere else in the world.'

Boris Becker, who was given a standing ovation, led by those in the Royal Box, after saying farewell as a competitor when he lost to Pat Rafter.

Although Boris Becker's 15th Wimbledon came to a disappointingly tame end in the shape of a backhand half-volley – one of the shots he used to play with such authority – landing in the tramlines, at least he said goodbye after 83 matches and 71 victories by losing to an opponent quite capable of one day adding his name to the honours board. Pat Rafter, the second seed, who had lost his two previous matches against the German, won 6–3, 6–2, 6–3 in an hour and 46 minutes.

'It's time to move on,' said Becker. 'Last time I said my retirement from Wimbledon was 99 per cent. Now it's 100 per cent. I've no regrets. I didn't expect to be in the last 16 playing Pat Rafter. He was a class better, but I'm thankful I had the chance to come back and play decent tennis. Now it's time to do something different.' He made a bold

enough start, breaking Rafter in the third game. But once he double-faulted to lose his own serve in the sixth game, the die was cast. It was an occasion to cherish inasmuch as there were reminders of that great athlete whose booming serves had helped him win more grass-court matches around the world (116) than any other active player. And there were plenty of crunching forehand service returns. But never enough. It was, as he said, time to move on.

Rafter, who then spent three hours 12 minutes partnering Jonas Bjorkman to a 7–6, 5–7, 3–6, 7–6, 6–4 defeat of teenagers Roger Federer from Switzerland and LLeyton Hewitt from Australia, had reached the last eight for the first time, where Todd Martin, an impressively efficient 7–6, 6–3, 6–4 winner over Goran Ivanisevic, was waiting for him. Both hit 24 aces, but once the

Below: Pat Rafter, quicker, sharper and now stronger, finally brought the curtain down on Boris Becker's Wimbledon career. And 'this time it's 100 per cent', said the German.

Nestor, losing only four points on serve in the first set and just two in the third. For good measure, he also hit 20 aces.

To make sure the five unresolved fourth-round matches in the ladies' singles were completed, they all began or resumed simultaneously. Steffi Graf, who had been within six points of reaching her tenth quarter-final when the rain interrupted her against qualifier Kim Cli-

Above: Alexandra Stevenson's latest strident display in beating Lisa Raymond earned her a quarter-final slot against fellow qualifier Jelena Dokic.

Croatian had lost the tie-break 7–5 and missed his one break point in the opening game of the second set, his challenge crumbled.

Pete Sampras, still to drop a set, continued his largely untroubled progress with a 6–3, 6–4, 6–2 win in 80 minutes over the Canadian left-hander, Daniel

jsters on Monday, took eight minutes to round off a 6–2, 6–2 victory. By then the exciting Croatian, Mirjana Lucic, had won the two games she needed to clinch success against Thailand's Tamarine Tanasugarn, while Alexandra Stevenson, 18, was on her way towards recovering from a nervous start for the 2–6, 7–6, 6–1 defeat of Lisa Raymond, which meant that, as she faced Jelena Dokic next, there would be a qualifier in the semi-finals for the first time.

Out on Court 18, Kournikova played sublimely in the first set against Williams, finding the requisite mixture of length and variety, but ultimately, and not for the first time, she was worn down by her opponent's greater weight of predictable, but damaging, shots and was beaten 3–6, 6–3, 6–2.

Venus Williams covered the court too well for Anna Kournikova.

Jonas Bjorkman poised at the net to try to cut off any return of the Pat Rafter's imminent serve (below). Champions past and present – Virginia Wade (opposite, top) in the 35 and over doubles, plus the dream mixed doubles team of Steffi Graf and John McEnroe (opposite, bottom) – also entertained the crowds.

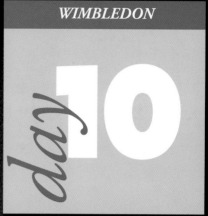

'That was probably the best match I've ever played which I have lost.'

Venus Williams underlining the rich quality of her much-interrupted quarter-final against former champion Steffi Graf.

Still the weather would not relent. Only two matches were completed, and although one of them, as Steffi Graf beat Venus Williams 6–2, 3–6, 6–4, was as fine a contest as one could wish to see, the day was again dominated by that infuriating drizzle, so thin that it did not even show up on the radar screen, but more than enough to make play impossible.

The day's obvious priority was to complete the ladies' singles quarter-finals, already running two days behind schedule. Provided they finished, there was still hope that the final could be played on Saturday on time. The loss of an hour at the start of the day was annoying, but did not look disastrous. It was only when it became another day of covers on, covers off and covers on again that the situation rapidly deteriorated.

At one stage it looked as if Lindsay Davenport's relatively straightforward 6–3, 6–4 defeat of defending champion Jana Novotna would be the only match

to finish. Then, approaching 7.30 p.m., by which time many had assumed there would be no further play, the rain did stop and the rush to complete the ladies' quarter-finals was on again.

Graf, trailing 1–2 in the final set, returned with Williams to Centre Court, but elsewhere a degree of chaos and farce developed as officials battled to make best use of the courts that were fit to resume. Although No. 1 Court was one of them, there was no point in bringing Tim Henman and Cedric Pioline back out when they had played only 13 points at the start of a best-of-five-sets match, especially as the other match in their half of the draw had already been postponed overnight. The only other men's singles quarter-final under way, between Patrick Rafter and Todd Martin, had stopped at 3–3 in the first set.

The initial thought was to switch Nathalie Tauziat's match with Mirjana Lucic there from Court 18, but when

Opposite: Steffi Graf at her imperious best as she eventually took charge in the final set to beat Venus Williams despite interruptions by the rain.

Lindsay Davenport won an often erratic quarter-final against defending champion Jana Novotna (opposite).

Jelena Dokic (below) was well on the way to wiping out Alexandra Stevenson's first-set advantage when the frustrating light rain halted their quarter-final until the next day.

the Croatian refused, the patiently waiting crowd on No. 1 Court was told there would be no further play. Imagine the surprise, then, when about 20 minutes later it was announced that an attempt to conclude the match between Jelena Dokic and Alexandra Stevenson, then poised at 3–6, 5–1 from Dokic's point of view, would be made there. This was because by the time No. 2 Court, where they should have continued, had been deemed still unplayable, the fans on No. 1 Court had already been sent home.

Hundreds scurried back when they heard what was happening, only for the rain to start again just as the players were warming up in the gloom, so the effort had to be aborted – and a Sunday final for the ladies then became certain. The weather had made it a nightmare for all concerned and yet the look of absolute joy on Graf's face as she completed her victory over Williams at least lit up Centre Court in a glorious manner. She came out in the gloom after a third break lasting two hours 39 minutes to

demonstrate what a great champion she remained.

The first break had been when Graf, who played superbly through most of the opening set, was trailing 2–3 on serve in the second. Then, after the American had taken the second set and was leading 1–0 in the third, off they had to go again. When they returned 90 minutes later, it was just for ten minutes, enough time for both players to hold serve once more and Graf to reach 40–15 in the fourth game with a gloriously won rally.

Many spectators had lost hope that it would be possible for them to finish that evening, but just after 7.30 p.m. the covers came off and the net went back up. At 7.43 p.m. Graf picked up where she had left off. A powerful serve followed by a rasping volley enabled her to hold for 2–2. In the end, experience was decisive. The crucial break came in the fifth game when Graf ended another of those pulsating side-to-side rallies that had gripped the crowd with a forehand winner down the line. Williams kept fighting. In an epic sixth game, Graf held after four deuces and, having saved three break points – seven hours after they had started, itself an hour late because of the rain – she served out in the tenth game to 30. Seldom had she looked so elated.

In the match to provide Graf with her next opponent, Nathalie Tauziat had taken the first set 6–4 against Mirjana Lucic and they were 3–3 in the second so, Graf apart, the only known semi-finalist was Davenport, whose bigger-serving, heavier-hitting tennis had ended the hopes of the defending champion, Jana Novotna. For such a significant outcome it was a pity the match had not been better, peppered, as it was, with unforced errors, not all of which could be blamed on the delays and interruptions.

Novotna, 0–5 against the American on other surfaces, made little impression until 1–3 in the second set, but although rallying to 3–3 never really looked as if she would be able to cling on to what she called 'the title which means the most'.

day **11**

It certainly was not the most compelling contest of the fortnight, but the wonderful opportunities that it kept alive meant that, in the eyes of many, Tim Henman's 6–4, 6–2, 4–6, 6–3 defeat of Cedric Pioline was one of the most important. For a second successive year, there was the real prospect of a British men's singles finalist at Wimbledon for the first time since Bunny Austin in 1938, and perhaps even the first British champion since Fred Perry's three-year reign was ended when he turned professional after retaining the title in 1936.

A year earlier such dreams had been broken by Pete Sampras. The American, a lucky beneficiary of an injury to Mark Philippoussis after the Australian had already tucked away the opening set, would also be blocking the way this time. Yet there was also a belief in the air that maybe, just maybe, this time Henman would produce the consistency coupled with the confidence to show that he could beat him on the tennis court as well as at golf.

'I'm obviously very pleased to win, but it was a very difficult match because I never really knew what to expect from my opponent,' said Henman. That was hardly surprising. Pioline has that lumbering, sometimes lugubrious approach that makes many wonder at times if he is even interested, except that, just when one is being convinced that he is not, he produces heavily spun service winners or groundstrokes right out of the top drawer.

Pioline, the only unseeded quarter-finalist, was immediately struggling when they took up where they had left off the day before. Henman, who had missed four break points, eventually took the first set with a scintillating backhand return, and another double fault, of which there were many from the Frenchman, also ended the second set.

By then Pioline also needed treatment for the consequences of a heavy fall a few games earlier but, as so often happens in such circumstances, he briefly bounced back in rejuvenated fashion, broke the British player and threatened

to make it a match by winning the third set. In some ways it was the jolt Henman needed, for he soon broke in the third by whipping another return to his opponent's shoelaces, but this was only the fourth among 18 break points that he had converted. The result was clearly more memorable than the performance, but afterwards, without actually shouting 'Bring on the champion', Henman was in suitably upbeat mood.

Tim Henman (opposite) was never seriously troubled in rounding off his interrupted quarter-final against Cedric Pioline (below) after only 13 points had been possible the previous day.

After Philippoussis had retired with a serious injury to his left knee when he was leading 6–4, 1–2, Sampras, who had reached this stage almost without needing to raise a sweat, was asked, 'Do you feel as if you dodged a bullet?' The American's dark eyebrows furrowed as he thought for a moment and then replied, 'Kind of. There's no question he was outplaying me, especially in the first set, even though I had chances to break. I was playing well, but he was coming up with some big, big serves and the way he was playing it was going to be tough to beat him.'

Philippoussis talked later about how, early in the second set, he heard an ominous click from his knee. 'At deuce, I hit a backhand passing shot down the line

and when I landed I sort of fell awkwardly. That's when I heard the click and grabbed it. I thought nothing of it until I jumped forward to return another serve and my knee just gave way and there was a huge click that time.' He heard another on the next point, realised that something probably serious was amiss and immediately decided to quit. The problem, it transpired, was a torn cartilage, which had not only ended his Wimbledon hopes, but also knocked him out of the Australian team to meet the United States in the centenary-celebrating Davis Cup match in Boston two weeks later.

The outcome of the two other quarter-finals gave what would be a semi-final between Andre Agassi and Patrick

Pete Sampras (opposite) knew only too well how lucky he had been when a knee injury forced Mark Philippoussis (below) to retire after he had overpowered the champion in the first set.

Rafter an added dimension, for it meant that the winner would take over as number one in the world rankings. Agassi, the fourth seed, had clearly relished the chance to take on the Brazilian, Gustavo Kuerten, who, despite winning matches at Wimbledon for the first time, never looked as if he had the weapons to disrupt the former champion, who beat him 6–3, 6–4, 6–4.

Indeed Agassi, who had persuaded officials to provide him with an umbrella under which to shelter from the sun during changeovers, was already going through his now familiar routine of blowing kisses to his fans by the time Rafter and Todd Martin, who had been 3–3 at the start of the day, reached one set all.

'Today was the best I've volleyed since I've been here and my returns were pretty solid,' said Rafter after his 6–3, 6–7, 7–6, 7–6 triumph. He had broken the Martin serve four times, which obviously pleased him, but dropped his own three times – a matter for some concern. Four of the service breaks came in the fourth set when Martin let Rafter escape twice in successive games.

In the two unfinished ladies' quarter-finals, the power and pace in 17-year-old Mirjana Lucic's fast-maturing game proved too much for 31-year-old Nathalie Tauziat, the runner-up one year earlier, while Alexandra Stevenson, 18, brought an end to an astonishing fortnight for the 16-year-old Australian, Jelena Dokic, in the battle to decide which of them would become the first qualifier in the history of The Championships to reach the semi-finals.

Stevenson, who had dominated the first set with her weighty driving from the back of the court the night before, but then drifted to 1–5 in the second, quickly returned to her original form on Court 1 once Dokic had accumulated the handful of points necessary to force a third set. It was not long before Stevenson was decisively ahead in the third, playing with a smile and authority that enabled her to win 6–3, 1–6, 6–3 and say, with teenage innocence, 'That was

fun. I've been waiting for this my whole life and it's very exciting.'

Out on Court 18, Nathalie Tauziat was left mourning the loss of a great opportunity to join Stevenson in the last four. She served for the match at 5–4 in the final set, but Lucic showed that she has strength of character as well as

Pat Rafter (opposite) was content with his form in beating Todd Martin (below) to reach his first Wimbledon semi-final.

strength of shot, and she suddenly launched a barrage of attacking groundstrokes and volleys that dramatically turned the match in her favour. Lucic won 4–6, 6–4, 7–5 to earn the right to challenge her heroine when she was learning to play. 'But she definitely won't be my hero in the semis,' she said firmly. Could she beat Graf? 'Everyone is beatable,' she said.

Meanwhile it was also a day for making headway and generally tidying up in the doubles and other events. Not surprisingly some of those still involved in singles and doubles felt it necessary to sacrifice their bids for more than one title. Rafter withdrew with Jonas Bjorkman from the quarter-finals of the men's doubles, and Lindsay Davenport with Todd Woodbridge did likewise to give John McEnroe and Steffi Graf a walkover into the last eight of the mixed, although Davenport maintained her in-

terest alongside Corina Morariu in the ladies' doubles, reaching the semi-finals with a 6–4, 7–6 defeat of Nicole Arendt and Manon Bollegraf.

Other leading doubles figures parted by more conventional means. The possibility of the Woodies (Todd Woodbridge and Mark Woodforde) reclaiming the men's doubles title, which had been their personal property for a record five years between 1993 and 1997, vanished when they were beaten 6–4, 5–7, 7–6, 6–4 by the new pairing of Jared Palmer and Paul Haarhuis. The latter, of course, had played his part in ending their run a year earlier when he and the now retired Jacco Eltingh beat them in the final. McEnroe and Graf were still in action, however, moving into the semi-finals with a 6–4, 6–3 victory over the Americans, Justin Gimelstob and Venus Williams, for whom it was their second match of the day.

Opposite: Mirjana Lucic's joy is clear for all to see after her quarter-final defeat of 1998 runner-up Nathalie Tauziat.

Below: Pressure builds on the Woodies, Todd Woodbridge (left) and Mark Woodforde, on their way to defeat by Jared Palmer and Paul Haarhuis.

*Above and opposite: Two classic shots that show
how serious Steffi Graf and John McEnroe were
about trying to win the mixed doubles.*

'It's just a matter of time before I really believe he breaks through and wins here. To win a Gra

Pete Sampras on Tim Henman's chances of one day wearing the Wimbledon singles crown.

m everything needs to fall into place, and he's going to be in contention still for several years.'

Pete Sampras: cool, calm and collected as he found a confident answer to Tim Henman's every challenge in their semi-final.

After such high British hopes, there was only domestic disappointment, doubtless felt most of all by Tim Henman himself, when he again failed to overcome his nemesis, Pete Sampras, for a place in the men's singles final. Instead the outcome of the day's principal contests decided that Sampras, the defending champion, would be seeking a modern-day record sixth title against Andre Agassi, while the ladies' singles final, a day later than planned, would be between the favourite, Steffi Graf, and an American slow to reveal the true depth of her talent, Lindsay Davenport.

Ever since Henman had gone closer than ever before, it seemed, to beating Sampras in the Stella Artois final at Queen's Club four weeks earlier, the expectation had been growing that the British number one was now at last ready to take that vital next step. It all started so well for him, although perhaps one should record that it all started so badly for the American. Sampras, just as he had done 24 hours earlier against Mark Philippoussis, served three double faults in the opening service game. And although he broke back, he was immediately broken again, which was enough to decide the opening set.

At 3–3 in the second set, Henman's chances looked even brighter. Sampras, apparently in pain, called for the trainer to rub embrocation into the top of his aching right thigh. One game later Sampras held his first break point. A backhand volley into the tramlines allowed Henman to escape . . . but the warning signs were starting to appear. Henman's control of his own service games was weakening and two woeful double faults as he served to remain in the set proved disastrous.

Sampras, who had at last found the smooth groove he had been seeking, began to take charge. The rare show of emotion after he also broke for 2–0 in the third set was a clear indication of his growing security, demonstrated again with the high kicking second serve with which he saved a break point in the fifth

game, and he went on to take the third set with the help of another Henman double fault. In six of seven service games spanning the end of the third set and the start of the fourth, Henman faced break points. That he saved so many was praiseworthy enough, but when he forced another break point in the fifth game of the fourth set, Sampras was more than ready to snatch it straight back.

It was Henman's last chance. At 4–4 he was broken to love. A scorching backhand pass down the line set up three break points. Another forceful return prompted a mistimed, overhit Henman volley and the outcome was then inevitable as Sampras applied the final touches one game later. 'I thought early on things were looking good for me, but on the day I lost to the better player,' said Henman. 'He definitely took his game up a level in the third set, but equally I know that I'm a better player than I was 12 months ago.'

Agassi ensured an all-American final on Independence Day when he barely offered Patrick Rafter the ghost of a chance as he swept to a 7–5, 7–6, 6–2 victory over the Australian. 'Who would have believed it a month ago?' asked an incredulous Agassi, who had barely had time to come to terms with the dramatic transformation in his life, as well as his form, after winning his first Grand Slam singles title for four years at the French Open.

He made barely half a dozen unforced errors as he drove Rafter close to the point of surrender. Whatever he tried, Agassi responded with something either quicker, sharper or both. One break of serve as Rafter fought in vain to deal with the length and rasping pace of Agassi's returns proved enough to decide the opening set, while a tie-break settled the second. There had been just one moment when Rafter might have found a way to change the momentum. He had two set points at 5–4 in the first set, but first another perfect-length, superbly timed forehand and then a smash lifted Agassi out of trouble.

One game later a double fault gave Agassi his first break point. He took it with a stunning backhand return, which forced Rafter to volley into the net. It was a scenario that was regularly repeated. The Australian continued to fight well enough in the second set, saving a break point in the fifth game and above all saving seven break points to hold for 5–4, but the effort required was beginning to take its toll. With nothing to lose, Rafter tried one bold gamble in the tie-break. At 1–2, he came charging to the net behind his serve, but his follow-up backhand volley went over the baseline. Agassi took the tie-break 7–5 and thereafter his confidence, like his returns, reached a magic level.

'That's the best I've seen him serve as well as return,' said Rafter. 'He was so strong from the baseline and never gave me a chance to control the points.' Agassi said, 'It's pretty amazing. It reflects a lot of hard work, but I'm far from satisfied. I feel I came here to win and there's still a lot of work for me to do.' Even so, such reticence could not mask the pleasure Agassi also felt about being one match away from becoming only the third player in Open tennis after Rod Laver in 1969 and Bjorn Borg (three times) to win the French and Wimbledon in the same year.

Above: Andre Agassi blows kisses to the crowd in a post-match ritual that has become his trademark.

Left: A pensive Pat Rafter comes to terms with his semi-final defeat by an opponent who was the better player on the day.

Similarly Graf, having endured quite a battering from the unranked Croatian, Mirjana Lucic, for an hour before experience pushed her through to a 6–7, 6–4, 6–3 victory, had earned the opportunity to achieve that clay-court/grass-court double for an amazing fifth time. Lucic was 17, Graf 30, but their hair, figures, facial features and game looked so similar that for both of them on Court No. 1, it must have seemed as if there was a near-mirror-image on the other side of the net.

Lucic certainly showed no signs of nerves as she took the game to her childhood heroine. She knew she had nothing to lose and proved it as she went for her shots with powerful relish as, both as a player and as a person, she was starting to bloom again after escaping the trauma of a childhood during which, she claimed, she had often been physically punished by her father. Not even Graf could cope with the flow of powerful forehand win-

ners from the teenager, who broke back when the German, in a first set that produced eight service breaks in the first ten games, served for it at 5–4. Lucic went on, after Graf saved two set points at 5–6, the first with an ace, the second with a reminder that her forehand was also still in fine working order after drawing her prey in with a delicate drop-shot, to dominate the tie-break 7–3.

The second set was just as intriguing. Lucic, who had practised that morning with John McEnroe, made Graf work for every point, continuing to take every chance to be aggressive until she had to try to fend off a set point at 4–5, 30–40. Disaster! She put what should have been an easy volley into the tramlines. Suddenly Graf's step quickened and her own shots stiffened. She won the first three games of the final set and that was too much for Lucic, although she had more than given due notice as to her beguiling prospects for the future.

Above: Mirjana Lucic, who, for a set and a half, had Steffi Graf on the ropes.

Opposite, top: No doubting whom these fans were supporting.

Opposite, bottom: The likenesses between them as Lucic and Graf come face to face are unmistakeable.

Below: However much damage her week of intensive practice, just before she flew to London, may have done to a friend's private grass court back home in California, Lindsay Davenport's form was clearly reaching a peak at precisely the right time.

By contrast Davenport had to take little more than a stroll in the sun, albeit a positive, no-nonsense one, to demolish 18-year-old Alexandra Stevenson 6–1, 6–1. Stevenson had already guaranteed herself £96,000 prize money – not bad for someone who began in the qualifying – to temper the pain of such a whopping defeat. The pattern had been set when Davenport won the first 11 points, and the sudden deflation of the Stevenson serve, which had provided the base for much of her earlier success, only added to the youngster's woes. Davenport's approach was powerful, inexorable and

above all ruthlessly efficient. The first set was over in 21 minutes, the second lasting just five minutes longer, and, having made her point so formidably on court, she made several more off it – mainly directed at Stevenson's mother.

'We don't appreciate her commenting on our way of life and especially calling all of us in some way a name,' said Davenport, determined not to use the word 'racist' herself. She said Alexandra was the nicest girl, with much talent, who did not need others to surround her with so much controversy.

The continued success by Leander

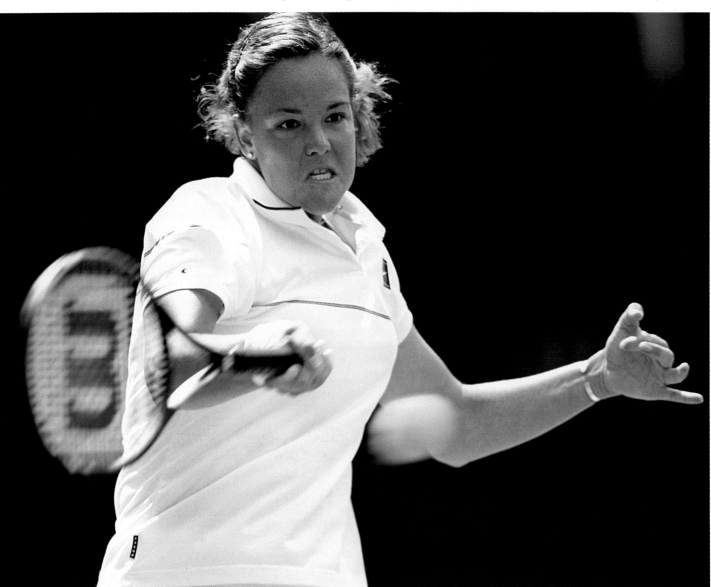

Paes and Mahesh Bhupathi, as they won a thrilling, marathon contest with Frenchmen Olivier Delaitre and Fabrice Santoro 2–6, 6–3, 7–6, 4–6, 7–5, meant that for the first time an Indian pair had reached the final of the men's doubles. It was an enthralling match, full of wonderful cut-and-thrust rallies before Bhupathi produced the shot of the contest with a fantastic lob on match point. Also through to the final after five gripping sets were Paul Haarhuis and Jared Palmer, who squeezed home 3–6, 7–5, 7–6, 4–6, 8–6 against Mark Knowles and Daniel Nestor.

After such a comfortable singles victory, Davenport had plenty of energy left as she and Corina Morariu reached the final of the ladies' doubles, 7–6, 6–3 against the unseeded Liezel Horn of South Africa and Katarina Srebotnik of Slovenia. In the final they would face another South African, Mariaan De Swardt, and Elena Tatarkova from the Ukraine, who upset Jana Novotna and Natasha Zvereva, both former champions with different partners, 6–4, 2–6, 7–5.

With Graf and John McEnroe withdrawing from the mixed doubles, so that the German could concentrate on the singles final, there was free passage for Jonas Bjorkman and Anna Kournikova into a final against opponents who were still to be decided.

Above: Alexandra Stevenson may have been outplayed, but still had reason to be happy with this winner.

Following pages: Anna Kournikova and Jonas Bjorkman on their way to the final of the mixed doubles.

At last . . . Victory for Lindsay Davenport (below, right) in singles – and in doubles with Corina Morariu (opposite).

Seldom in recent years have there been finer examples in the two singles finals of the respective champions keeping their best to last. First Lindsay Davenport unveiled a powerful command of the whole court under pressure, which she had never revealed before on the Centre Court, to take the ladies' singles title, 6–4, 7–5, against Steffi Graf. Then Pete Sampras produced a level of awesome grass-court tennis that not even he had achieved in winning five previous finals to retain the crown, 6–3, 6–4, 7–5, against former champion Andre Agassi.

They were two splendid finals that

was clear not only that she could, but that they were precisely the tactics she was determined to use against the German.

It was never an exciting final because the pattern was set right from the start when Davenport, having chosen to receive, broke at her second opportunity with a backhand service-return winner down the line and then saved a break point against her to hold for 2–0. Effectively that was the first set decided there and then, but the waywardness evident in Graf's game was also due in no small measure to the relentless pressure that her opponent's walloping shots applied. Davenport has never played better.

Graf opened the second set with her most positive service game so far and for a moment, when she reached a break-point chance by courtesy of some rare Davenport unforced errors, one wondered if her renowned capacity for survival was about to click into operation again. Davenport put paid to such ideas with another devastating winner down the line and that was that. All the extra fitness work she had undertaken to shed those surplus pounds, which coach Robert Van't Hof kept telling her were holding her back, suddenly became worthwhile as she waltzed on with a relaxed freedom few display in their first Wimbledon final.

For once Graf was unable to dictate the pattern of the points. She was the one under attack. Not even a 29-minute interruption for rain, when she was 30–15 serving to make it 5–5, gave Davenport more than a flicker of concern. She held to 30, forced a break point with another fierce return in the next game, took it by working her way to the net in a rally to put away a forehand cross-court volley in the way Graf used to do, and then served out on her second match point with a service winner.

Wiping away tears of joy, Davenport, the only competitor this year to play seven matches without yielding a set, said, 'I've struggled on this surface for so long. I never thought Wimbledon would be a tournament I could win.'

'I made my decision before the match. I won't be back as a player . . . and nothing will change my mind. I didn't wave goodbye to the crowd because it was Lindsay's day and I wanted to keep it at that.'

Steffi Graf, the seven-times champion, beaten in her ninth final, announcing her retirement from Wimbledon.

swept away the memories of all the frustrations and complications created by the weather during two bouts of rain in the second week, as another record crowd watched nine hours of almost unbroken play and the five major and six supporting competitions were all completed on time – all but one of them changing hands.

Uppermost in the minds of many as Graf, with her left thigh supported by a protective strapping, prepared to face Davenport was whether the American would be able to counter her penetrating groundstrokes, especially off the forehand, into the corners. Within minutes it

Then, hugging the silver plate, the reigning US Open and Olympic champion, who also knew that a day later she would be reinstated as number one in the women's world rankings, said, 'It's the most beautiful trophy I've ever seen. I can't believe I've done it. I'll pick being Wimbledon champion over being number one any day.'

The American dignitaries in particular in the Royal Box on the Fourth of July just could not lose. Nor, with the quality of tennis they were about to admire in the first all-American men's singles final since Jim Courier lost to Sampras, of course, in 1993, could the crowd. By common consent, Agassi remained the best returner of the serve in the game. Twenty-four hours earlier he had looked invincible against Patrick Rafter. Yet over the next hour and 55 minutes, although he produced flashes of brilliance and certainly had chances, especially in the first set, Agassi's defences were ripped apart in the most merciless fashion by a man who seldom had been more worthy of his nickname, 'Pistol Pete'.

Agassi was confidence personified at the start, not content with a quickstep between points, but taking off on a positive jog to his chair for changeovers. His first chance to break came in the third game when his ferocious treatment of a second serve must have left Sampras wondering why he had bothered to deliver it in the first place. In true Sampras fashion, though, he just brushed his brow, twitched his right shoulder, took aim and sent down an ace. In the seventh game another series of flashing returns left Agassi holding three break points. His opponent's response remained devastating – four ferocious service winners followed by an ace on second serve. 'The more you attack me, the more likely you are to get burned,' seemed to be Sampras's message to him. And to rub it home, Sampras promptly broke in the next game with the help of a double fault, served out for the set and took 23 of the next 26 points. 'In six minutes I'd gone from 3–3, 0–40 to a set and a break down,' Agassi reflected almost disbelievingly later. 'But that's how Pete plays. He can turn a whole match round in a minute and a half.'

Thereafter, although it was not until the 11th game that Sampras broke in the third set, after Agassi had twice escaped with winning serves of his own in the seventh, Sampras's tennis was almost faultless. There was a final touch of resistance from Agassi when he played one amazing forehand cross-court winner from deep in his own forehand corner, which left Sampras with a grazed arm from his despairing full-length leap, but then it was ace 16 to match point and ace 17 to become champion for a sixth time.

It had been the performance of a maestro. Bjorn Borg won five years in succession between 1976 and 1980, but no one, since the abolition of the Challenge Round, has won so often. It was also Sampras's 12th Grand Slam singles title, enabling him to draw level with Roy Emerson's all-time record, and, according to Agassi, there will surely be

Opposite: Pete Sampras was in unbeatable form, even at full stretch.

Below: Andre Agassi tried all he knew to break down Sampras's conrol.

Following pages: Sampras launches into that brilliant serve, full of variety and guile, which is so often the foundation of his success.

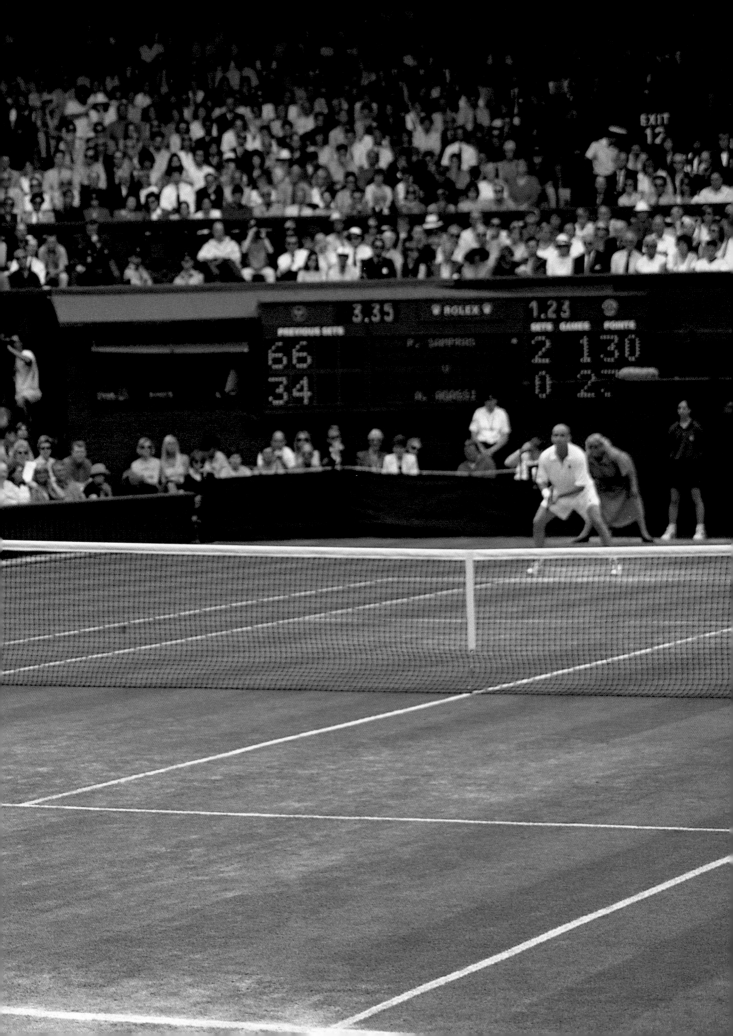

more to come. 'If he wants to come back and win again, then he can do so for the next four years,' said the runner-up, for whom a return to number one in the rankings was scant consolation. 'The fact that I've risen to number one again is fine, but today on Centre Court at Wimbledon I was not number one.'

While all this was taking place, out on Court 3, Mahesh Bhupathi and Leander Paes were following up their success in becoming the first Indian winners at the French Open by matching that achievement at Wimbledon. 'For us to win Wimbledon has always been a dream and one we never thought would come true,' said Bhupathi, who revealed that he had played throughout the fortnight with torn abdominal muscles from an earlier tournament, which had been progressively limiting him.

They beat Paul Haarhuis, the 1998 champion with Jacco Eltingh, and Jared Palmer 6–7, 6–3, 6–4, 7–6. Several hours later, in his third match of the day, his second in the mixed doubles, Paes, a former junior boys' singles winner, collected a second title when he and Lisa Raymond combined too athletically for Jonas Bjorkman and Anna Kournikova, whose double-faulting problems returned, 6–4, 3–6, 6–3. They not only collected the trophy, but they also pocketed the balls as additional mementoes of a great day.

Davenport was also a double winner when she and Corina Morariu combined to beat Mariaan De Swardt and Elena Tatarkova 6–4, 6–4 on Court 1. It brought Davenport's prize money at the end of the fortnight to £497,935 from 26 sets. For the record, Sampras earned £455,000 from playing 21 sets.

A misunderstanding over the time at which his semi-final was due to start meant that David Nalbandian, the Argentinian second seed, lost the chance of a place in the boys' singles final against top-seeded Kristian Pless, the only Dane at The Championships this year. The Austrian, Jurgen Melzer, who was the beneficiary of the muddle, took full ad-

vantage for he went on to beat Pless 7–6, 6–3. Earlier in the week the best British effort had come from Scotland's Alan Mackin, who upset seventh-seeded Thiago Alves of Brazil in the first round and only lost to Nalbandian 7–5 in the third in the quarter-finals.

There was some consolation for Nalbandian in the boys' doubles. He and fellow countryman Guillermo Coria, who had beaten two British pairs, Lee Childs and Simon Dickson and then Mark Hilton and James Nelson, earlier in the day, fought off growing exhaustion to defeat Todor Enev of Bulgaria and Jarkko Nieminen of Finland 7–5, 6–4.

Uzbekistan, which in 1998 showed more TV hours of Wimbledon (166) than the BBC (163), produced its first Wimbledon winner. Iroda Tulyaganova beat the Russian, Lina Krasnoroutskai, 7–6, 6–4, in the girls' singles final but, partnered by the Ukrainian, Tetiana Perebiynis, was overcame 6–1, 2–6, 6–2 in the doubles final by Daniela Bedanova of the Czech Republic and Maria Salerni of Argentina.

As for the veteran invitation events, Ken Flach and Robert Seguso, winners of the main men's doubles title in 1987, showed that they had lost none of their competitive flair by beating Peter McNamara and Paul McNamee, both also former doubles champions, 6–3, 3–6, 9–7 for the 35 and over title, while in the 45 and overs Brian Gottfried and Tom Gullikson beat two other top doubles exponents of their day, Ross Case and Geoff Masters, 6–1, 7–6.

In the ladies' 35 and over invitation, those wily Australians, Liz Smylie and Wendy Turnbull, not only went through their three round-robin group matches without losing a set, but then in the final beat the American, Gretchen Magers, and Holland's Betty Stove, runner-up in singles, doubles and mixed in 1977, 7–5, 6–3. Betty could have been forgiven for thinking, 'It was ever thus.'

Opposite: Mahesh Bhupathi (left) and Leander Paes, the popular first Indian winners of the gentlemen's doubles title.

Below: Champions for the future? Junior singles winners Iroda Tulyaganova and Jurgen Melzer.

The Ladies' Doubles Championship
Corina Morariu & Lindsay Davenport

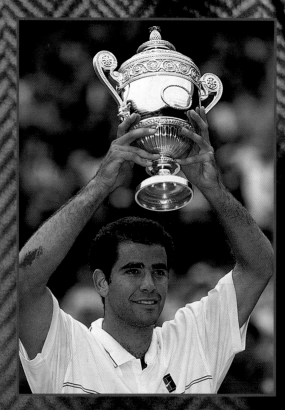

The Gentlemen's Singles Championship
Pete Sampras

The Mixed Doubles Championship
Leander Paes & Lisa Raymond

The 35 and over Gentlemen's Invitation Doubles
Ken Flach & Robert Seguso

The 35 and over Ladies' Invitation Doubles
Liz Smylie & Wendy Turnbull

The Boys' Doubles Championship
Guillermo Coria & David Nalbandian

The Ladies' Singles Championship
Lindsay Davenport

The Gentlemen's Doubles Championship
Leander Paes & Mahesh Bhupathi

The Girls' Singles Championship
Iroda Tulyagonova

The Girls' Doubles Championship
Maria-Emilia Salerni & Daniela Bedanova

The Boys' Singles Championship
Jurgen Melzer

The 45 and over Gentlemen's Invitation Doubles
Tom Gullikson & Brian Gottfried

CHAMPIONSHIP RECORDS

1999

LADIES

Abe Miss J. *(Germany)*
Adams Miss K.M. *(USA)*
66 Ahl Miss L.A. *(Great Britain)*
55 Appelmans Miss S. *(Belgium)*
41 Arendt Miss N. *(USA)*
45 Bacheva Miss L. *(Bulgaria)*
24 Barabanschikova Miss O. *(Belarus)*
Barclay Miss C.G. *(Australia)*
Bes Miss E. *(Spain)*
61 Black Miss C. *(Zimbabwe)*
Bollegraf Miss M.M. *(Netherlands)*
77 Boogert Miss K. *(Netherlands)*
13 Brandi Miss K. *(USA)*
39 Callens Miss E.S.H. *(Belgium)*
72 Capriati Miss J. *(USA)*
26 Carlsson Miss A. *(Sweden)*
127 Cervanova Miss L. *(Slovak Republic)*
99 Chi Miss J. *(USA)*
83 Chladkova Miss D. *(Czech Republic)*
118 Clijsters Miss K. *(Belgium)*
40 Cocheteux Miss A. *(France)*
113 Coetzer Miss A.J. *(South Africa)*
124 Courtois Miss L. *(Belgium)*
23 Cristea Miss C. *(Romania)*
Crook Miss H. *(Great Britain)*
120 Cross Miss K.M. *(Great Britain)*
33 Davenport Miss L.A. *(USA)*
Davies Miss V.E. *(Great Britain)*
De Beer Miss S. *(South Africa)*
91 De Lone Miss E.R. *(USA)*
126 de Swardt Miss M. *(South Africa)*
De Villiers Miss N. *(South Africa)*
46 Dechaume-Balleret Mrs A. *(France)*
54 Dechy Miss N. *(France)*
79 Dementieva Miss E. *(Russia)*
Dhenin Miss C. *(France)*
89 Diaz Oliva Miss M. *(Argentina)*
2 Dokic Miss J. *(Australia)*
105 Dragomir Miss R. *(Romania)*
85 Drake Miss M. *(Canada)*
Ellwood Miss A. *(Australia)*
20 Farina Miss S. *(Italy)*
6 Fernandez Miss M.J. *(USA)*
31 Foldenyi Miss A. *(Hungary)*
21 Frazier Miss A. *(USA)*
Freye Miss K. *(Germany)*
34 Fusai Miss A. *(France)*
110 Gagliardi Miss E. *(Switzerland)*
30 Glass Miss A. *(Germany)*
38 Golarsa Miss L. *(Italy)*
107 Gorrochategui Miss I. *(Argentina)*
128 Graf Miss S. *(Germany)*
Graham Miss D.A. *(USA)*
14 Grande Miss R. *(Italy)*
73 Grzybowska Miss M. *(Poland)*
121 Guse Miss K-A. *(Australia)*
35 Habsudova Miss K. *(Slovak Republic)*
17 Halard-Decugis Mrs J. *(France)*
1 Hingis Miss M. *(Switzerland)*
Hiraki Miss R. *(Japan)*
67 Hopmans Miss A. *(Netherlands)*
Horn Miss L. *(South Africa)*
88 Hrdlickova Miss K. *(Czech Republic)*
71 Huber Miss A. *(Germany)*
Husarova Miss J. *(Slovak Republic)*
59 Jeyaseelan Miss S. *(Canada)*
Jidkova Miss A. *(Russia)*
Kim Miss E. *(Korea Republic)*
68 Kleinova Miss S. *(Czech Republic)*
86 Koulikovskaya Miss E. *(Russia)*
112 Kournikova Miss A. *(Russia)*
5 Kremer Miss A. *(Luxemburg)*
Krizan Miss T. *(Slovenia)*
117 Kruger Miss J. *(South Africa)*
Kunce Mrs K. *(Australia)*
28 Kuti-Kis Miss R. *(Hungary)*
Labat Miss F. *(Argentina)*
Landa Miss M. F. *(Argentina)*
104 Latimer Miss L. *(Great Britain)*
122 Lee Miss J. *(Chinese Taipei)*
47 Leon Garcia Miss G. *(Spain)*
44 Li Miss F. *(China P.R.)*
76 Likhovtseva Miss E. *(Russia)*
4 Loit Miss E. *(France)*
92 Lucic Miss M. *(Croatia)*
Lugina Miss O. *(Ukraine)*
Marosi Miss K. *(Hungary)*
Martincova Miss E. *(Czech Republic)*
27 Martinez Miss C. *(Spain)*
McNeil Miss L.M. *(USA)*
McQuillan Miss R. *(Australia)*
McShea Miss L. *(Australia)*
Melicharova Miss E. *(Czech Republic)*
Menga Miss V. *(Brazil)*
Miyagi Miss N. *(Japan)*
75 Molik Miss A. *(Australia)*
Montalvo Miss L. *(Argentina)*
123 Morariu Miss C. *(USA)*
Muric Miss M. *(Croatia)*
18 Nacuk Miss S. *(Yugoslavia)*
52 Nagyova Miss H. *(Slovak Republic)*
43 Neiland Mrs L. *(Latvia)*
69 Nejedly Miss J. *(Canada)*
Nemeckova Miss L. *(Czech Republic)*
70 Noorlander Miss S. *(Netherlands)*
64 Novotna Miss J. *(Czech Republic)*
Olsza Miss A. *(Poland)*
98 Oremans Miss M. *(Netherlands)*
Ortuno Miss A. *(Spain)*
119 Osterloh Miss L. *(USA)*
51 Panova Miss T. *(Russia)*
115 Papadaki Miss C. *(Greece)*
60 Petrova Miss N. *(Russia)*
16 Pierce Miss M. *(France)*
Pisnik Miss T. *(Slovenia)*
102 Pitkowski Miss S. *(France)*
Pleming Miss L. *(Australia)*
62 Plischke Miss S. *(Austria)*
50 Po Miss K. *(USA)*
114 Pratt Miss N.J. *(Australia)*
Probst Miss W. *(Germany)*
82 Pullin Miss J.M. *(Great Britain)*
29 Raymond Miss L.M. *(USA)*
Reeves Miss S. *(USA)*
8 Rippner Miss B. *(USA)*
84 Rittner Miss B. *(Germany)*
9 Ruano Pascual Miss V. *(Spain)*
78 Rubin Miss C. *(USA)*
116 Saeki Miss M. *(Japan)*
57 Sanchez Lorenzo Miss M.A. *(Spain)*
32 Sanchez Vicario Miss A. *(Spain)*
Schaerer Miss L. *(Paraguay)*
48 Schett Miss B. *(Austria)*
Schlukebir Miss K. *(USA)*
53 Schnyder Miss P. *(Switzerland)*
111 Schwartz Miss B. *(Austria)*
96 Seles Miss M. *(USA)*
Selyutina Miss I. *(Kazakhstan)*
42 Serna Miss M. *(Spain)*
19 Serra-Zanetti Miss A. *(Italy)*
10 Shaughnessy Miss M. *(USA)*
103 Sidot Miss A-G. *(France)*
Singer Miss C. *(Germany)*
90 Smashnova Miss A. *(Israel)*
108 Smith Miss S. *(Great Britain)*
25 Snyder Miss T. *(USA)*
7 Spirlea Miss I. *(Romania)*
101 Srebotnik Miss K. *(Slovenia)*
Steck Miss J. *(South Africa)*
22 Stevenson Miss A. *(USA)*
Stewart Miss B. *(Australia)*
37 Stoyanova Miss P. *(Bulgaria)*
Stubbs Miss R.P. *(Australia)*
3 Studenikova Miss K. *(Slovak Republic)*
106 Suarez Miss P. *(Argentina)*
74 Sugiyama Miss A. *(Japan)*
56 Talaja Miss S. *(Croatia)*
87 Tanasugarn Miss T. *(Thailand)*
Tarabini Miss P. *(Argentina)*
100 Tatarkova Miss E. *(Ukraine)*
65 Tauziat Miss N. *(France)*
81 Testud Miss S. *(France)*
12 Tordoff Miss A. *(Great Britain)*
95 Torrens-Valero Miss C. *(Spain)*
80 Van Roost Mrs D. *(Belgium)*
109 Vento Miss M.A. *(Venezuela)*
Vildova Miss H. *(Czech Republic)*
Vis Miss C.M. *(Netherlands)*
11 Wagner Mrs E. *(Germany)*
63 Wang Miss S-T. *(Chinese Taipei)*
93 Ward Miss J. *(Great Britain)*
Washington Miss M. *(USA)*
125 Watanabe Miss J. *(USA)*
94 Weingartner Miss M. *(Germany)*
58 Wild Miss L. *(USA)*
97 Williams Miss V. *(USA)*
36 Woodroffe Miss L.A. *(Great Britain)*
Yoshida Miss Y. *(Japan)*
15 Zuluaga Miss F. *(Colombia)*
49 Zvereva Miss N. *(Belarus)*

GENTLEMEN

Adams D. *(South Africa)*
96 Agassi A. *(USA)*
119 Alami K. *(Morocco)*
Albano P. *(Argentina)*
7 Alonso J. *(Spain)*
105 Arazi H. *(Morocco)*
Ardinghi M. *(Italy)*
85 Arthurs W. *(Australia)*
Bale L. *(South Africa)*
Barnard M. *(South Africa)*
115 Becker B. *(Germany)*
Bertolini M. *(Italy)*
Bhupathi M. *(India)*
125 Bjorkman J. *(Sweden)*
58 Black B. *(Zimbabwe)*
4 Black W. *(Zimbabwe)*
5 Blanco G. *(Spain)*
Bowen D. *(USA)*
Braasch K. *(Germany)*
Brandi C. *(Italy)*
Broad N. *(Great Britain)*
Bryan B. *(USA)*
Bryan M. *(USA)*
93 Canas G. *(Argentina)*
127 Caratti C. *(Italy)*
Carbonell T. *(Spain)*
Carrasco J. *(Spain)*
Childs L. *(Great Britain)*
28 Clavet F. *(Spain)*
39 Clement A. *(France)*
Coetzee J. *(South Africa)*
19 Costa A. *(Spain)*
Coupe B. *(USA)*
52 Courier J. *(USA)*
51 Cowan B. *(Great Britain)*
37 Damm M. *(Czech Republic)*
De Jager J-L. *(South Africa)*
Del Rio D. *(Argentina)*
Delaitre O. *(France)*
60 Delgado J. *(Great Britain)*
59 Delgado R. *(Paraguay)*
63 Di Pasquale A. *(France)*
Dickson S. *(Great Britain)*
Dilucia D. *(USA)*
Djordjevic N. *(Yugoslavia)*
90 Dosedel S. *(Czech Republic)*
2 Draper S. *(Australia)*
98 Dreekmann H. *(Germany)*
92 El Aynaoui Y. *(Morocco)*
Ellwood B. *(Australia)*
123 Enqvist T. *(Sweden)*
100 Federer R. *(Switzerland)*
Ferreira A. *(Brazil)*
Ferreira E. *(South Africa)*
53 Ferreira W. *(South Africa)*
118 Filippini M. *(Uruguay)*
Flach D. *(USA)*
Florent A. *(Australia)*
83 Fromberg R. *(Australia)*
Galbraith P. *(USA)*
71 Gambill J. *(USA)*
21 Gaudio G. *(Argentina)*
103 Gimelstob J. *(USA)*
Godwin N. *(South Africa)*
Goellner M-K. *(Germany)*
14 Goldstein P. *(USA)*
Grabb J. *(USA)*
Grant G. *(USA)*
Greenhalgh J. *(New Zealand)*
57 Grosjean S. *(France)*
91 Gross O. *(Germany)*
124 Gumy H. *(Argentina)*
84 Gustafsson M. *(Sweden)*
106 Haarhuis P. *(Netherlands)*
81 Haas T. *(Germany)*
Hadad A. *(Israel)*
Haggard C. *(South Africa)*
Haygarth B. *(South Africa)*
64 Henman T. *(Great Britain)*
47 Hernandez A. *(Mexico)*
117 Hewitt L. *(Australia)*
Hill M. *(Australia)*
101 Hipfl M. *(Austria)*
Hood M. *(Argentina)*
30 Hrbaty D. *(Slovak Republic)*
Humphries S. *(USA)*
54 Ilie A. *(Australia)*
112 Ivanisevic G. *(Croatia)*
25 Johansson T. *(Sweden)*
Johnson D. *(USA)*
33 Kafelnikov Y. *(Russia)*
12 Karbacher B. *(Germany)*
Keil M. *(USA)*
Kempers T. *(Netherlands)*
113 Kiefer N. *(Germany)*
Kitinov A. *(Macedonia)*
104 Knippschild J. *(Germany)*
Knowles M. *(Bahamas)*
Koenig R. *(South Africa)*
27 Kohlmann M. *(Germany)*
Kokavec B. *(Canada)*
10 Koubek S. *(Austria)*
Koves G. *(Hungary)*
65 Krajicek R. *(Netherlands)*
Kratzmann A. *(Australia)*
50 Kroslak J. *(Slovak Republic)*
48 Kucera K. *(Slovak Republic)*
80 Kuerten G. *(Brazil)*
Kulti N. *(Sweden)*
88 Lapentti N. *(Ecuador)*
3 Lareau S. *(Canada)*
34 Larsson M. *(Sweden)*
Leach R. *(USA)*
94 Lee M. *(Great Britain)*
Lopez-Moron A. *(Spain)*
116 MacLagan M. *(Great Britain)*
Macpherson D. *(Australia)*
MacPhie B. *(USA)*
31 Malisse X. *(Belgium)*
108 Mamiit C. *(USA)*
69 Manta L. *(Switzerland)*
16 Mantilla F. *(Spain)*
75 Marin J. A. *(Costa Rica)*
121 Marques N. *(Portugal)*
89 Martin A. *(Spain)*
97 Martin T. *(USA)*
McEnroe J.P. *(USA)*
11 Medvedev A. *(Ukraine)*
Merklein M. *(USA)*
Middleton T.J. *(USA)*
23 Milligan L. *(Great Britain)*
Mirnyi M. *(Belarus)*
Montana F. *(USA)*
Motomura G. *(Japan)*
49 Moya C. *(Spain)*
Navarra M. *(Italy)*
9 Nestor D. *(Canada)*
Nicolas E. *(Spain)*
22 Norman M. *(Sweden)*
Norval P. *(South Africa)*
99 Novak J. *(Czech Republic)*
Nyborg P. *(Sweden)*
O'Brien A. *(USA)*
Oncins J. *(Brazil)*
46 Paes L. *(India)*
Palmer J. *(USA)*
20 Parmar A. *(Great Britain)*
95 Pavel A. *(Romania)*
74 Pescariu D. *(Romania)*
Pescosolido S. *(Italy)*
32 Philippoussis M. *(Australia)*
38 Pioline C. *(France)*
40 Portas A. *(Spain)*
43 Pozzi G. *(Italy)*
Prieto S. *(Argentina)*
78 Prinosil D. *(Germany)*
Puentes G. *(Spain)*
128 Rafter P. *(Australia)*
Ran E. *(Israel)*
36 Raoux G. *(France)*
26 Reneberg R.A. *(USA)*
Rikl D. *(Czech Republic)*
Roberts D. *(South Africa)*
Roditi D. *(Mexico)*
77 Rodriguez M. *(Argentina)*
Rosner P. *(South Africa)*
102 Rosset M. *(Switzerland)*
17 Rusedski G. *(Great Britain)*
66 Ruud C. *(Norway)*
45 Sa A. *(Brazil)*
1 Sampras P. *(USA)*
Sanchez J. *(Spain)*
56 Sanguinetti D. *(Italy)*
86 Santopadre V. *(Italy)*
24 Santoro F. *(France)*
8 Sapsford D.E. *(Great Britain)*
62 Sargsian S. *(Armenia)*
55 Schalken S. *(Netherlands)*
122 Schuttler R. *(Germany)*
Sell M. *(USA)*
Sherwood D. *(Great Britain)*
13 Siemerink J. *(Netherlands)*
Silcock G. *(Australia)*
15 Spadea V. *(USA)*
70 Spinks T. *(Great Britain)*
72 Squillari F. *(Argentina)*
35 Srichaphan P. *(Thailand)*
126 Stafford G. *(South Africa)*
67 Stanoytchev O. *(Bulgaria)*
Stark J. *(USA)*
Stepanek R. *(Czech Republic)*
110 Stolle S. *(Australia)*
18 Stoltenberg J. *(Australia)*
Suk C. *(Czech Republic)*
6 Suzuki T. *(Japan)*
76 Tarango J. *(USA)*
Tebbutt M. *(Australia)*
120 Tieleman L. *(Italy)*
111 Tillstrom M. *(Sweden)*
Tramacchi P. *(Australia)*
Trifu G. *(Romania)*
42 Ulihrach B. *(Czech Republic)*
Ullyett K. *(South Africa)*
41 Vacek D. *(Czech Republic)*
109 Van Lottum J. *(Netherlands)*
Vanhoudt T. *(Belgium)*
Velasco J. *(Spain)*
107 Vicente F. *(Spain)*
114 Vinck C. *(Germany)*
Vizner P. *(Czech Republic)*
87 Voinea A. *(Romania)*
44 Voltchkov V. *(Belarus)*
Waite J. *(USA)*
82 Wessels P. *(Netherlands)*
Whitehouse W. *(South Africa)*
79 Wilkinson C. *(Great Britain)*
68 Woodbridge T.A. *(Australia)*
29 Woodforde M. *(Australia)*
61 Woodruff C. *(USA)*
73 Zimonjic N. *(Yugoslavia)*

GIRLS

62 Abram Miss A. *(Poland)*
9 Abramovic Miss I. *(Croatia)*
14 Adamczak Miss M. *(Australia)*
51 Aoyama Miss K. *(Japan)*
3 Babakova Miss M. *(Slovak Republic)*
41 Baker Miss L. *(New Zealand)*
54 Baltacha Miss E. *(Great Britain)*
25 Bao Miss L. *(Switzerland)*
11 Barnes Miss A. *(Great Britain)*
35 Barnes Miss R. *(Great Britain)*
53 Barnikow Miss L. *(USA)*
19 Basu Miss C.A. *(Germany)*
33 Bedanova Miss D. *(Czech Republic)*
21 Benesova Miss I. *(Czech Republic)*
6 Berecz Miss K. *(Hungary)*
5 Birnerova Miss E. *(Czech Republic)*
40 Bovina Miss E. *(Russia)*
26 Camerin Miss M.E. *(Italy)*
24 Cargill Miss A. *(USA)*
18 Carter Miss C. *(Great Britain)*
38 Castro Miss V. *(Chile)*
43 Charbonnier Miss C. *(Switzerland)*
27 Collin Miss H. *(Great Britain)*
29 Culum Miss N. *(Slovenia)*
32 Danilidou Miss E. *(Greece)*
55 Dlhopolcova Miss L. *(Slovak Republic)*
44 Dowse Miss M. *(Australia)*
10 Farr Miss H. *(Great Britain)*
23 Fokina Miss G. *(Russia)*
15 Gerards Miss M. *(Netherlands)*
63 Grandin Miss N. *(South Africa)*
57 Granville Miss L. *(USA)*
Gregg Miss S. *(Great Britain)*
Hawkins Miss A. *(Great Britain)*
31 Hergold Miss T. *(Slovenia)*
48 Kapros Miss A. *(Hungary)*
34 Keothavong Miss A. *(Great Britain)*
49 Krasnoroutskai Miss L. *(Russia)*
52 Krauth Miss E. *(Argentina)*
28 Krauth Miss V. *(Argentina)*
58 Krishnamurthy Miss K. *(Canada)*
36 Krstulovic Miss D. *(Croatia)*
37 Kurhajcova Miss L. *(Slovak Republic)*
59 Luzarova Miss D. *(Czech Republic)*
22 Mojzis Miss A. *(South Africa)*
39 Muller Miss M. *(Germany)*
50 Nikolaeva Miss A. *(Belarus)*
60 Pennetta Miss F. *(Italy)*
8 Perebiynis Miss T. *(Ukraine)*
1 Rafolomana Miss A. *(Madagascar)*
13 Rencken Miss N. *(South Africa)*
30 Resch Miss B. *(Austria)*
45 Reyes Miss Z. *(Mexico)*
12 Reynolds Miss D. *(Mexico)*
16 Salerni Miss M.E. *(Argentina)*
7 Scaringe Miss J. *(USA)*
46 Seal Miss C. *(Great Britain)*
2 Smith Miss J. *(Great Britain)*
Stone Miss S. *(Australia)*
4 Stosur Miss S. *(Australia)*
47 Trinder Miss N. *(Great Britain)*
17 Tulyaganova Miss I. *(Uzbekhistan)*
64 Uda Miss R. *(Japan)*
42 Vinci Miss R. *(Italy)*
20 Vymetal Miss K. *(Great Britain)*
61 Wallace Miss C. *(Great Britain)*
Webley-Smith Miss E. *(Great Britain)*
56 Werner Miss S. *(Germany)*
Wood Miss L. *(Great Britain)*

BOYS

29 Abel M. *(Germany)*
49 Alves T. *(Brazil)*
61 Ancic M. *(Croatia)*
Anderson A. *(South Africa)*
53 Banks A. *(Great Britain)*
19 Beck K. *(Slovak Republic)*
56 Becker B. *(Germany)*
8 Benneteau J. *(France)*
30 Berke S. *(USA)*
36 Bogomolov A. *(USA)*
46 Britzen D. *(Germany)*
10 Brooks R. *(Great Britain)*
60 Childs L. *(Great Britain)*
41 Chramosta L. *(Czech Republic)*
17 Coria G. *(Argentina)*
Davis T. *(USA)*
16 De Armas J. *(Venezuela)*
28 Dickson S. *(Great Britain)*
63 Enev T. *(Bulgaria)*
22 Faurel J-C. *(France)*
40 Fish M. *(USA)*
Francis A. *(USA)*
45 Froberg J. *(Sweden)*
Fruttero J-P. *(USA)*
55 Furukawa H. *(Japan)*
13 Gard C. *(Romania)*
Gray J. *(Great Britain)*
Green R. *(Great Britain)*
18 Greenhouse N. *(Great Britain)*
11 Gremelmayr D. *(Germany)*
39 Hammer P. *(Germany)*
27 Harboe P. *(Chile)*
58 Harper-Griffith L. *(USA)*
14 Hasek J. *(Czech Republic)*
51 Hemmes F. *(Netherlands)*
Higgins T. *(Great Britain)*
42 Hilton M.A. *(Great Britain)*
25 Johansson J. *(Sweden)*
4 Karanusic R. *(Croatia)*
62 Kiendl U. *(Germany)*
43 Kracman A. *(Slovenia)*
2 Lammer M. *(Switzerland)*
20 Langre D. *(Mexico)*
50 Mackin A. *(Great Britain)*
54 Mahut N. *(France)*
5 Martin D. *(USA)*
52 McDade A. *(South Africa)*
59 Meffert D. *(Germany)*
34 Melzer J. *(Austria)*
37 Miyazaki Y. *(Japan)*
64 Nalbandian D. *(Argentina)*
38 Nelson J. *(Great Britain)*
33 Nieminen J. *(Finland)*
6 Nieminen T. *(Finland)*
12 Nugent S. *(Eire)*
44 Ormaza M. *(Argentina)*
47 Pampoulov L. *(Austria)*
1 Pless K. *(Denmark)*
48 Prodon E. *(France)*
31 Riby B. *(Great Britain)*
24 Roddick A. *(USA)*
57 Rojer J-J. *(Netherland Antillies)*
3 Russell R. *(Jamaica)*
15 Stegmann D. *(South Africa)*
7 Thys R. *(Belgium)*
21 Trudgeon M. *(Great Britain)*
9 Villagran C. *(Argentina)*
26 Vlaski A. *(Yugoslavia)*
35 Weaver M. *(Great Britain)*
Weir-Smith B. *(South Africa)*
23 Wong W. *(Hong Kong)*
32 Zovko L. *(Croatia)*

Bold figures denote position in Singles Draw

The winner becomes the holder, for the year only, of the CHALLENGE CUP presented by The All England Lawn Tennis and Croquet Club. The winner receives a silver replica of the Challenge Cup. A silver salver is presented to the runner-up and a bronze medal to each defeated semi-finalist.

Holder: P.Sampras

First Round	Second Round	Third Round	Fourth Round	Quarter-Finals	Semi-Finals	Final
1. P.Sampras [1] ....(USA)	P.Sampras [1] 6/3 6/4 6/4	P.Sampras [1] 6/4 6/2 6/3	P.Sampras [1] 6/3 6/4 7/5	P.Sampras [1] 6/3 6/4 6/2	P.Sampras [1] 4/6 2/1 Ret'd	P.Sampras [1] 3/6 6/4 6/3 6/4
2. S.Draper ....(AUS)						
3. S.Lareau ....(CAN)	S.Lareau 6/1 3/6 6/3 6/3					
4. W.Black ....(ZIM)						
5. G.Blanco ....(ESP)	G.Blanco .....6/4 3/6 7/6(4) 7/6(7)	D.E.Sapsford 6/3 3/6 6/4 6/2				
6. T.Suzuki ....(JPN)						
7. J.Alonso ....(ESP)	D.E.Sapsford 6/2 6/2 7/5					
(Q) 8. D.E.Sapsford ....(GBR)						
9. D.Nestor ....(CAN)	D.Nestor 6/2 6/3 6/4	D.Nestor 6/1 7/5 6/3	D.Nestor .....6/3 6/7(3) 6/0 6/7(4) 6/4			
10. S.Koubek ....(AUT)						
11. A.Medvedev ....(UKR)	A.Medvedev ....7/6(1) 7/6(3) 6/4					
12. B.Karbacher ....(GER)						
13. J.Siemerink ....(NED)	P.Goldstein 6/4 5/7 4/6 6/2 6/1	P.Goldstein ......6/2 6/4 6/7(5) 6/2				
14. P.Goldstein ....(USA)						
15. V.Spadea ....(USA)	F.Mantilla [16] ..7/6(2) 7/6(4) 4/6 7/6(7)					
16. F.Mantilla [16] ....(ESP)						
17. G.Rusedski [9] ....(GBR)	G.Rusedski [9] 6/1 6/4 6/2	G.Rusedski [9] ....6/3 6/4 7/6(3)	G.Rusedski [9] 6/3 6/4 7/5			
18. J.Stoltenberg ....(AUS)						
19. A.Costa ....(ESP)	A.Parmar ......0/6 7/6(5) 6/3 6/3					
(Q) 20. A.Parmar ....(GBR)						
21. G.Gaudio ....(ARG)	M.Norman 6/4 7/5 7/5	M.Norman ....6/2 6/3 7/6(5)				
22. M.Norman ....(SWE)						
(W) 23. L.Milligan ....(GBR)	F.Santoro ....6/4 7/5 7/6(0)					
24. F.Santoro ....(FRA)						
25. T.Johansson ....(SWE)	T.Johansson ...5/7 7/6(5) 6/3 4/6 6/1	F.Clavet 4/6 1/6 6/1 6/3 6/4	M.Philippoussis [7] ...2/6 7/6(4) 6/3 6/1	M.Philippoussis [7]		
(Q) 26. R.A.Reneberg ....(USA)						
(L) 27. M.Kohlmann ....(GER)	F.Clavet 6/2 1/6 3/6 7/5 6/4					
28. F.Clavet ....(ESP)						
29. M.Woodforde ....(AUS)	M.Woodforde 6/4 6/2 6/2	M.Philippoussis [7] ...6/7(4) 7/6(6) 7/6(5) 6/2				
30. D.Hrbaty ....(SVK)						
31. X.Malisse ....(BEL)	M.Philippoussis [7] .6/7(4) 6/3 6/3 6/4					
32. M.Philippoussis [7] ....(AUS)						
33. Y.Kafelnikov [3] ....(RUS)	Y.Kafelnikov [3] .6/7(4) 7/5 7/6(4) 4/6 7/5	Y.Kafelnikov [3] .....6/7(3) 6/4 7/6(4) 6/4	C.Pioline ....3/6 6/4 1/0 Ret'd	C.Pioline .....6/4 5/7 7/6(5) 4/6 6/3	T.Henman [6] 6/4 6/2 4/6 6/3	
34. M.Larsson ....(SWE)						
(Q) 35. P.Srichaphan ....(THA)	P.Srichaphan ......6/2 6/4 7/6(7)					
36. G.Raoux ....(FRA)						
37. M.Damm ....(CZE)	C.Pioline ....7/6(7) 6/4 6/2	C.Pioline 6/3 6/1 6/3				
38. C.Pioline ....(FRA)						
39. A.Clement ....(FRA)	A.Clement 6/3 6/2 6/4					
40. A.Portas ....(ESP)						
41. D.Vacek ....(CZE)	D.Vacek 6/1 6/2 6/4	D.Vacek ....4/6 6/3 7/6(6) 5/7 6/3	K.Kucera [13] ......6/1 6/3 3/6 7/6(4)			
42. B.Ulihrach ....(CZE)						
43. G.Pozzi ....(ITA)	G.Pozzi ....7/6(6) 6/2 6/2					
44. V.Voltchkov ....(BLR)						
(Q) 45. A.Sa ....(BRA)	A.Sa ....6/4 6/4 7/6(4)	K.Kucera [13] ....7/6(4) 6/3 6/2				
46. L.Paes ....(IND)						
(Q) 47. A.Hernandez ....(MEX)	K.Kucera [13] 6/2 6/1 6/2					
48. K.Kucera [13] ....(SVK)						
49. C.Moya [12] ....(ESP)	C.Moya [12] 6/4 7/5 6/2	J.Courier ....6/3 3/6 7/6(1) 3/6 6/2	J.Courier .....7/6(2) 3/6 3/6 7/5 13/11	T.Henman [6] ...4/6 7/5 7/5 6/7(5) 9/7		
50. J.Kroslak ....(SVK)						
(W) 51. B.Cowan ....(GBR)	J.Courier 6/3 6/4 6/4					
52. J.Courier ....(USA)						
53. W.Ferreira ....(RSA)	A.Ilie .....7/6(13) 7/5 6/7(10) 6/1	S.Schalken 6/4 6/1 2/6 6/3				
54. A.Ilie ....(AUS)						
55. S.Schalken ....(NED)	S.Schalken .....5/7 6/4 7/6(5) 7/5 6/3					
56. D.Sanguinetti ....(ITA)						
57. S.Grosjean ....(FRA)	S.Grosjean 5/7 6/0 7/5 7/5	S.Grosjean ....6/2 6/2 7/6(2)	T.Henman [6] ...6/1 6/7(8) 6/3 6/2			
58. B.Black ....(ZIM)						
59. R.Delgado ....(PAR)	J.Delgado 6/2 6/1 7/5					
(Q) 60. J.Delgado ....(GBR)						
61. C.Woodruff ....(USA)	C.Woodruff ....6/3 3/6 6/3 6/7(7) 6/2	T.Henman [6] ....6/4 6/3 7/6(4)				
62. S.Sargsian ....(ARM)						
63. A.Di Pasquale ....(FRA)	T.Henman [6] 6/4 6/0 3/6 6/1					
64. T.Henman [6] ....(GBR)						
65. R.Krajicek [5] ....(NED)	R.Krajicek [5] 6/2 6/3 6/1	R.Krajicek [5] 7/5 6/4 6/4	L.Manta ......6/3 7/6(5) 4/6 4/6 6/4	G.Kuerten [11] 7/5 6/4 5/7 6/3	A.Agassi [4] 6/3 6/4 6/4	
66. C.Ruud ....(NOR)						
67. O.Stanoytchev ....(BUL)	T.A.Woodbridge ...6/3 6/7(4) 6/4 6/7(5) 10/8					
68. T.A.Woodbridge ....(AUS)						
(Q) 69. L.Manta ....(SUI)	L.Manta ....6/7(5) 7/6(3) 7/6(2) 6/2	L.Manta ....6/4 6/4 3/6 6/7(4) 6/3				
(W) 70. T.Spinks ....(GBR)						
71. J.Gambill ....(USA)	J.Gambill ......6/1 6/3 7/6(5)					
72. F.Squillari ....(ARG)						
(Q) 73. N.Zimonjic ....(YUG)	N.Zimonjic .....7/6(4) 7/6(3) 6/7(6) 6/4	N.Zimonjic ....7/6(5) 1/6 6/3 7/6(6)	G.Kuerten [11] 6/4 6/4 6/2			
74. D.Pescariu ....(ROM)						
75. J. A.Marin ....(CRC)	J.Tarango 6/4 6/1 7/5					
76. J.Tarango ....(ARG)						
77. M.Rodriguez ....(ARG)	D.Prinosil ....7/5 6/4 7/6(5)	G.Kuerten [11] 6/3 6/3 6/2				
78. D.Prinosil ....(GER)						
(W) 79. C.Wilkinson ....(GBR)	G.Kuerten [11] 7/5 6/4 6/4					
80. G.Kuerten [11] ....(BRA)						
81. T.Haas [14] ....(GER)	T.Haas [14] 3/6 6/4 4/6 6/3 6/4	T.Haas [14] ......6/7(4) 4/6 6/4 6/3 6/2	W.Arthurs ......7/6(6) 7/6(3) 7/6(2)	A.Agassi [4] ...6/7(5) 7/6(5) 6/1 6/4		
82. P.Wessels ....(NED)						
83. R.Fromberg ....(AUS)	R.Fromberg ....6/4 7/6(1) 6/3					
84. M.Gustafsson ....(SWE)						
(Q) 85. W.Arthurs ....(AUS)	W.Arthurs ....7/6(7) 6/7(5) 7/6(10) 7/6(4)	W.Arthurs ....7/5 7/6(7) 7/5				
86. V.Santopadre ....(ITA)						
87. A.Voinea ....(ROM)	N.Lapentti .....7/6(8) 6/3 4/6 2/6 8/6					
88. N.Lapentti ....(ECU)						
89. A.Martin ....(ESP)	A.Martin .....7/6(8) 6/4 2/6 6/7(3) 10/8	A.Martin 6/2 3/6 7/5 6/3				
90. S.Dosedel ....(CZE)						
91. O.Gross ....(GER)	Y.El Aynaoui ....6/1 4/6 7/6(3) 6/4					
92. Y.El Aynaoui ....(MAR)						
93. G.Canas ....(ARG)	G.Canas 4/6 6/3 6/2 1/6 9/7	A.Agassi [4] 6/3 6/4 6/3	A.Agassi [4] 6/2 6/0 2/6 6/3			
(W) 94. M.Lee ....(GBR)						
95. A.Pavel ....(ROM)	A.Agassi [4] 6/1 6/2 6/4					
96. A.Agassi [4] ....(USA)						
97. T.Martin [8] ....(USA)	T.Martin [8] ...6/7(6) 6/7(5) 6/3 6/2 6/4	T.Martin [8] ....7/6(5) 6/4 6/4	T.Martin [8] ....6/7(5) 6/1 7/6(6) 7/5	T.Martin [8] ......7/6(3) 6/3 6/4	P.Rafter [2] 6/3 6/7(5) 7/6(5) 7/6(3)	
98. H.Dreekmann ....(GER)						
99. J.Novak ....(CZE)	J.Novak 6/3 3/6 4/6 6/3 6/4					
(W)100. R.Federer ....(SUI)						
101. M.Hipfl ....(AUT)	M.Rosset 6/4 5/7 3/6 6/3 6/2	J.Knippschild 6/3 6/4 6/4				
102. M.Rosset ....(SUI)						
103. J.Gimelstob ....(USA)	J.Knippschild ...6/3 2/6 5/7 6/2 9/7					
104. J.Knippschild ....(GER)						
105. H.Arazi ....(MAR)	P.Haarhuis ......7/6(4) 6/3 6/2	P.Haarhuis 6/2 6/2 6/2	G.Ivanisevic [10] ...7/6(2) 6/4 7/6(3)			
106. P.Haarhuis ....(NED)						
107. F.Vicente ....(ESP)	F.Vicente 3/6 6/2 2/6 7/5 6/3					
108. C.Mamiit ....(USA)						
109. J.Van Lottum ....(NED)	S.Stolle ....7/6(8) 6/3 6/1	G.Ivanisevic [10] ...7/6(8) 4/6 4/6 6/4				
(Q) 110. S.Stolle ....(AUS)						
(Q) 111. M.Tillstrom ....(SWE)	G.Ivanisevic [10] 6/4 6/3 6/4					
112. G.Ivanisevic [10] ....(CRO)						
113. N.Kiefer [15] ....(GER)	N.Kiefer [15] ....2/6 6/4 6/3 7/6(4)	B.Becker 6/4 6/2 6/4	B.Becker ......6/1 6/4 7/6(5)	P.Rafter [2] 6/3 6/2 6/3		
(Q) 114. C.Vinck ....(GER)						
115. B.Becker ....(GER)	B.Becker .....5/7 6/7(5) 6/4 7/6(5) 6/4					
(W)116. M.MacLagan ....(GBR)						
117. L.Hewitt ....(AUS)	L.Hewitt 6/2 6/2 6/1	L.Hewitt 6/1 6/4 4/6 6/4				
(W)118. M.Filippini ....(URU)						
119. K.Alami ....(MAR)	K.Alami 6/1 6/4 6/4					
120. L.Tieleman ....(ITA)						
(Q) 121. N.Marques ....(POR)	R.Schuttler 6/1 6/4 6/4	T.Enqvist 6/2 6/4 7/5	P.Rafter [2] ....7/6(5) 6/3 6/2			
122. R.Schuttler ....(GER)						
123. T.Enqvist ....(SWE)	T.Enqvist ....6/1 6/4 7/6(2)					
124. H.Gumy ....(ARG)						
125. J.Bjorkman ....(SWE)	J.Bjorkman 6/4 6/1 6/4	P.Rafter [2] ....6/2 7/6(3) 6/7(7) 6/2				
(Q) 126. G.Stafford ....(RSA)						
(Q) 127. C.Caratti ....(ITA)	P.Rafter [2] 6/3 6/2 6/2					
128. P.Rafter [2] ....(AUS)						

Heavy type denotes seeded players. The figure in brackets against names denotes the order in which they have been seeded. (W) = Wild card. (Q) = Qualifier. (L) = Lucky loser.

The matches are the best of five sets

The winners become the holders, for the year only, of the CHALLENGE CUPS presented by the OXFORD UNIVERSITY LAWN TENNIS CLUB and the late SIR HERBERT WILBERFORCE respectively. The winners receive silver replicas of the two Challenge Cups. A silver salver is presented to each of the runners-up, and a bronze medal to each defeated semi-finalist.

Holders: J.Eltingh and P.Haarhuis

First Round	Second Round	Third Round	Quarter-Finals	Semi-Finals	Final

1. **M.Bhupathi** (IND) & **L.Paes** (IND) ....[1]
2. T.Kempers (NED) & M.Kohlmann (GER) ....
(Q) 3. B.Kokavec (CAN) & G.Trifu (ROM)
4. A.Martin (ESP) & E.Ran (ISR)
5. J.Grabb (USA) & D.Johnson (USA)
6. M.Hill (AUS) & P.Nyborg (SWE) ....
7. M.Ardinghi (ITA) & A.Lopez-Moron (ESP) ....
8. **P.Galbraith** (USA) & **J.Gimelstob** (USA) ....[16]
9. **S.Lareau** (CAN) & **A.O'Brien** (USA) ....[9]
10. M.Hood (ARG) & S.Prieto (ARG)
11. G.Koves (HUN) & R.Stepanek (CZE)
12. D.Bowen (USA) & M.Sell (USA)
(W) 13. L.Childs (GBR) & S.Dickson (GBR)
14. B.Bryan (USA) & M.Bryan (USA)
15. G.Grant (USA) & T.J.Middleton (USA)
16. **E.Ferreira** (RSA) & **R.Leach** (USA) ....[7]
17. **W.Black** (ZIM) & **S.Stolle** (AUS) ....[4]
18. S.Humphries (USA) & J.Waite (USA)
19. N.Godwin (RSA) & M.Keil (USA)
(Q) 20. M.Navarra (ITA) & S.Pescosolido (ITA)
(W) 21. M.MacLagan (GBR) & A.Parmar (GBR)
(W) 22. B.Cowan (GBR) & W.Whitehouse (RSA)
23. B.MacPhie (USA) & J.Tarango (USA)
24. **D.Prinosil** (GER) & **D.Vacek** (CZE) ....[14]
25. **M.Damm** (CZE) & **C.Suk** (CZE) ....[11]
26. D.Rikl (CZE) & S.Schalken (NED)
27. N.Broad (GBR) & R.Koenig (RSA)
28. D.Flach (USA) & M-K.Goellner (GER)
29. P.Tramacchi (AUS) & P.Vizner (CZE)
(Q) 30. A.Ferreira (BRA) & G.Motomura (JPN)
31. E.Nicolas (ESP) & G.Puentes (ESP)
32. **O.Delaitre** (FRA) & **F.Santoro** (FRA) ....[5]
33. **M.Knowles** (BAH) & **D.Nestor** (CAN) ....[6]
34. N.Marques (POR) & T.Vanhoudt (BEL)
35. K.Braasch (GER) & C.Haggard (RSA)
36. D.Del Rio (ARG) & M.Rodriguez (ARG)
(W) 37. D.Sherwood (GBR) & T.Spinks (GBR)
38. R.A.Reneberg (USA) & J.Stark (USA)
39. M.Bertolini (ITA) & C.Brandi (ITA)
40. **W.Arthurs** (AUS) & **A.Kratzmann** (AUS) ....[12]
41. **N.Kulti** (SWE) & **M.Tillstrom** (SWE) ....[13]
(W) 42. R.Federer (SUI) & L.Hewitt (AUS)
43. B.Coupe (USA) & M.Merklein (USA)
(W) 44. D.E.Sapsford (GBR) & C.Wilkinson (GBR)
45. P.Albano (ARG) & T.Carbonell (ESP)
46. B.Black (ZIM) & W.Ferreira (RSA)
47. M.Barnard (RSA) & B.Haygarth (RSA)
48. **J.Bjorkman** (SWE) & **P.Rafter** (AUS) ....[3]
49. **P.Haarhuis** (NED) & **J.Palmer** (USA) ....[8]
50. J.Greenhalgh (NZL) & G.Silcock (USA)
51. A.Florent (AUS) & D.Macpherson (AUS)
52. A.Kitinov (MKD) & F.Montana (USA)
53. N.Lapentti (ECU) & J.Sanchez (ESP)
54. D.Dilucia (USA) & P.Rosner (RSA)
(L) 55. A.Hadad (ISR) & D.Roberts (RSA)
56. **D.Adams** (RSA) & **J-L.De Jager** (RSA) ....[10]
57. **P.Norval** (RSA) & **K.Ullyett** (RSA) ....[15]
58. N.Djordjevic (YUG) & N.Zimonjic (YUG)
59. P.Goldstein (USA) & D.Roditi (MEX)
60. L.Bale (RSA) & G.Stafford (RSA)
61. G.Kuerten (BRA) & J.Oncins (BRA)
62. Y.Kafelnikov (RUS) & M.Mirnyi (BLR)
63. J.Carrasco (ESP) & J.Velasco (ESP)
64. **T.A.Woodbridge** (AUS) & **M.Woodforde** (AUS) ....[2]

Second Round

M.Bhupathi & L.Paes [1] ....6/4 6/2 7/6(3)
B.Kokavec & G.Trifu ....6/3 6/4 7/6(5)
J.Grabb & D.Johnson ....6/4 7/6(4) 7/6(2)
P.Galbraith & J.Gimelstob [16] 6/0 6/2 6/4
S.Lareau & A.O'Brien [9] 6/1 6/4 1/6 6/3
D.Bowen & M.Sell ....6/4 2/4 Ret'd
B.Bryan & M.Bryan ....6/3 7/5 7/6(6)
E.Ferreira & R.Leach [7] ....7/5 7/6(5) 7/6(1)
W.Black & S.Stolle [4] ....6/4 6/7(6) 6/1
M.Navarra & S.Pescosolido ....6/3 6/4 7/6(0)
B.Cowan & W.Whitehouse 6/4 6/3 6/3
B.MacPhie & J.Tarango ....6/4 5/7 3/6 7/6(5) 6/4
D.Rikl & S.Schalken ....6/3 6/4 6/7(2) 5/7 6/4
N.Broad & R.Koenig 4/6 6/3 7/5 6/4
P.Tramacchi & P.Vizner 4/6 6/4 7/5 6/3
O.Delaitre & F.Santoro [5] 6/1 6/3 6/1
M.Knowles & D.Nestor [6] 6/3 7/5 6/1
K.Braasch & C.Haggard ....7/6(2) 7/5 6/3
R.A.Reneberg & J.Stark ....6/2 6/1 6/7(8) 7/6(3)
W.Arthurs & A.Kratzmann [12] ....4/6 7/6(6) 6/4 7/5
R.Federer & L.Hewitt ....4/6 6/3 7/6(3) 6/7(4) 6/4
B.Coupe & M.Merklein ....6/3 7/6(4) 6/3
P.Albano & T.Carbonell 7/5 4/6 7/5 5/7 8/6
J.Bjorkman & P.Rafter [3] 6/1 4/6 4/6 6/3 6/3
P.Haarhuis & J.Palmer [8] 7/5 6/1 6/4
A.Florent & D.Macpherson ....7/6(4) 4/6 6/4 6/3
D.Dilucia & P.Rosner ....6/3 7/6(8) 6/7(4) 6/2
D.Adams & J-L.De Jager [10] 6/3 6/2 6/4
P.Norval & K.Ullyett [15] 4/6 6/1 6/3 3/6 10/8
L.Bale & G.Stafford 6/4 6/4 6/3
Y.Kafelnikov & M.Mirnyi 2/6 6/4 6/4 2/6 14/12
T.A.Woodbridge & M.Woodforde [2] ....7/6(5) 6/2 6/4

Third Round

M.Bhupathi & L.Paes [1] ....7/5 7/6(3) 6/3
P.Galbraith & J.Gimelstob [16] ....7/6(12) 6/7(4) 6/3 6/2
S.Lareau & A.O'Brien [9] ....2/6 6/1 6/3 7/6(3)
B.Bryan & M.Bryan ....6/3 5/7 7/6(3) 6/3
W.Black & S.Stolle [4] 7/5 6/3 6/3
B.Cowan & W.Whitehouse ....6/7(3) 6/3 7/6(4) 7/6(5)
N.Broad & R.Koenig 6/4 4/6 5/7 6/2 6/3
O.Delaitre & F.Santoro [5] 6/4 3/6 6/3 1/6 6/3
M.Knowles & D.Nestor [6] ....3/6 7/6(5) 6/4 7/5
R.A.Reneberg & J.Stark 6/3 7/5 3/6 4/6 7/5
R.Federer & L.Hewitt ....6/4 7/6(1) 6/3
J.Bjorkman & P.Rafter [3] 7/5 6/3 6/4
P.Haarhuis & J.Palmer [8] ....3/6 7/6(6) 7/6(3) 7/6(3)
D.Adams & J-L.De Jager [10] 6/3 6/2 6/4
P.Norval & K.Ullyett [15] ....7/5 6/7(7) 6/2 7/6(4)
T.A.Woodbridge & M.Woodforde [2] ....w/o

Quarter-Finals

M.Bhupathi & L.Paes [1] 6/4 4/6 6/4 6/4
S.Lareau & A.O'Brien [9] 4/6 6/4 6/2 4/6 10/8
W.Black & S.Stolle [4] ....6/4 7/6(3) 6/3
O.Delaitre & F.Santoro [5] 6/4 4/6 6/4 7/5
M.Knowles & D.Nestor [6] ....7/6(7) 6/3 6/4
J.Bjorkman & P.Rafter [3] ....7/6(1) 5/7 3/6 7/6(3) 6/4
P.Haarhuis & J.Palmer [8] ....7/6(3) 6/2 6/1
T.A.Woodbridge & M.Woodforde [2] 4/6 6/4 6/3 6/3

Semi-Finals

M.Bhupathi & L.Paes [1] ....3/6 4/6 7/6(5) 6/4 6/4
O.Delaitre & F.Santoro [5] 5/7 6/4 6/2 7/5
M.Knowles & D.Nestor [6] ....w/o
P.Haarhuis & J.Palmer [8] ....3/6 7/5 7/6(4) 4/6 8/6

Final

M.Bhupathi & L.Paes [1] ....2/6 6/3 7/6(5) 4/6 7/5
M.Bhupathi & L.Paes [1] ....6/7(10) 6/3 6/4 7/6(4)

Holder: Miss J.Novotna

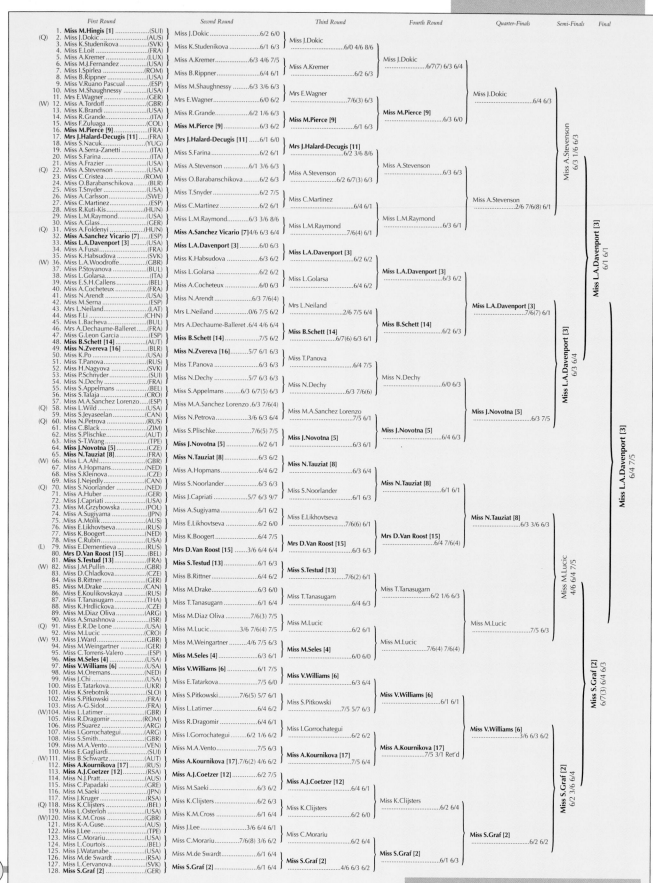

First Round	Second Round	Third Round	Fourth Round	Quarter-Finals	Semi-Finals	Final
1. **Miss M.Hingis [1]** ....(SUI)	Miss J.Dokic 6/2 6/0					
(Q) 2. Miss J.Dokic ....(AUS)		Miss J.Dokic				
3. Miss K.Studenikova ....(SVK)	Miss K.Studenikova 6/1 6/3					
4. Miss E.Loit ....(FRA)		....................6/0 4/6 8/6				
5. Miss A.Kremer ....(LUX)	Miss A.Kremer 6/3 4/6 7/5		Miss J.Dokic			
6. Miss M.J.Fernandez ....(USA)		Miss A.Kremer				
7. Miss I.Spirlea ....(ROM)	Miss B.Rippner 6/4 6/1	......................6/2 6/3	......................6/7(7) 6/3 6/4			
8. Miss B.Rippner ....(USA)						
9. Miss V.Ruano Pascual ....(ESP)	Miss M.Shaughnessy ...6/3 3/6 6/3			Miss J.Dokic		
10. Miss M.Shaughnessy ....(USA)		Mrs E.Wagner				
11. Mrs E.Wagner ....(GER)	Mrs E.Wagner 6/0 6/2	......................7/6(3) 6/2				
(W) 12. Miss A.Tordoff ....(GBR)			Miss M.Pierce [9]	......................6/4 6/3		
13. Miss K.Brandi ....(USA)	Miss R.Grande 6/2 1/6 6/1					
14. Miss R.Grande ....(ITA)		**Miss M.Pierce [9]**	......................6/3 6/0			
15. Miss F.Zuluaga ....(COL)	**Miss M.Pierce [9]** 6/3 6/2					
16. **Miss M.Pierce [9]** ....(FRA)		......................6/1 6/3				
17. **Mrs J.Halard-Decugis [11]** ..(FRA)	Mrs J.Halard-Decugis [11] 6/1 6/0					
18. Miss S.Nacuk ....(YUG)		Mrs J.Halard-Decugis [11]				
19. Miss A.Serra-Zanetti ....(ITA)	Miss S.Farina 6/2 6/1					
20. Miss S.Farina ....(ITA)		......................6/2 3/6 8/6			Miss A.Stevenson	
21. Miss A.Frazier ....(USA)	Miss A.Stevenson 6/1 3/6 6/3		Miss A.Stevenson		6/3 1/6 6/3	
(Q) 22. Miss A.Stevenson ....(USA)		Miss A.Stevenson				
23. Miss C.Cristea ....(ROM)	Miss O.Barabanschikova ...6/2 6/3	......................6/2 6/7(3) 6/3				
24. Miss O.Barabanschikova .....(BLR)						
25. Miss T.Snyder ....(USA)	Miss T.Snyder 6/2 7/5		......................6/3 6/1			
26. Miss A.Carlsson ....(SWE)		Miss C.Martinez		Miss A.Stevenson		
27. Miss C.Martinez ....(ESP)	Miss C.Martinez 6/2 6/1					
28. Miss R.Kuti-Kis ....(HUN)		......................6/4 6/1		....................2/6 7/6(8) 6/1		
29. Miss L.M.Raymond ....(USA)	Miss L.M.Raymond 6/3 3/6 8/6		Miss L.M.Raymond			
30. Miss A.Glass ....(GER)		Miss L.M.Raymond				
(Q) 31. Miss A.Foldenyi ....(HUN)	**Miss A.Sanchez Vicario [7]** 4/6 6/3 6/4		......................6/3 6/1			
32. **Miss A.Sanchez Vicario [7]** .(ESP)		......................7/6(4) 6/1				
33. **Miss L.A.Davenport [3]** ....(USA)	**Miss L.A.Davenport [3]** 6/0 6/3					
34. Miss A.Fusai ....(FRA)		**Miss L.A.Davenport [3]**				
35. Miss K.Habsudova ....(SVK)	Miss K.Habsudova 6/3 6/2		**Miss L.A.Davenport [3]**			
(W) 36. Miss L.A.Woodroffe ....(GBR)		......................6/2 6/2				
37. Miss P.Stoyanova ....(BUL)	Miss L.Golarsa 6/2 6/2		......................6/3 6/2			
38. Miss L.Golarsa ....(ITA)		Miss L.Golarsa				
39. Miss E.S.H.Callens ....(BEL)	Miss A.Cocheteux 6/0 6/3					
40. Miss A.Cocheteux ....(FRA)		......................6/4 6/2		**Miss L.A.Davenport [3]**		
41. Miss N.Arendt ....(USA)	Miss N.Arendt ....6/3 7/6(4)			....................7/6(7) 6/1		
42. Miss M.Serna ....(ESP)		Mrs L.Neiland				
43. Mrs L.Neiland ....(LAT)	Mrs L.Neiland 0/6 7/5 6/2					
44. Miss F.Li ....(CHN)		......................2/6 7/5 6/4				**Miss L.A.Davenport [3]**
45. Miss L.Bacheva ....(BUL)	Mrs A.Dechaume-Balleret .6/4 4/6 6/4		Miss B.Schett [14]			6/1 6/1
46. Mrs A.Dechaume-Balleret .....(FRA)		**Miss B.Schett [14]**				
47. Miss G.Leon Garcia ....(ESP)	**Miss B.Schett [14]** 7/5 6/3		......................6/2 6/3			
48. **Miss B.Schett [14]** ....(AUT)		......................6/7(6) 6/3 6/1				
49. **Miss N.Zvereva [16]** ....(BLR)	**Miss N.Zvereva [16]** 5/7 6/1 6/3					
50. Miss K.Po ....(USA)		Miss T.Panova				
51. Miss T.Panova ....(RUS)	Miss T.Panova 6/3 6/3					
52. Miss H.Nagyova ....(SVK)		......................6/4 7/5				
53. Miss P.Schnyder ....(SUI)	Miss N.Dechy 5/7 6/3 6/3		Miss N.Dechy			
54. Miss N.Dechy ....(FRA)		Miss N.Dechy				
55. Miss S.Appelmans ....(BEL)	Miss S.Appelmans ....6/3 6/7(5) 6/3		......................6/0 6/3			
56. Miss S.Talaja ....(CRO)		......................6/3 7/6(6)		Miss J.Novotna [5]		
57. Miss M.A.Sanchez Lorenzo ...(ESP)	Miss M.A.Sanchez Lorenzo .6/3 7/6(4)			......................6/3 7/5		
(Q) 58. Miss L.Wild ....(USA)		Miss M.A.Sanchez Lorenzo				
59. Miss S.Jeyaseelan ....(CAN)	Miss N.Petrova 3/6 6/3 6/4					
(Q) 60. Miss N.Petrova ....(RUS)		......................7/5 6/1				
61. Miss C.Black ....(ZIM)	Miss S.Plischke ....7/6(5) 7/5		Miss J.Novotna [5]			
62. Miss S.Plischke ....(AUT)		**Miss J.Novotna [5]**				
63. Miss S-T.Wang ....(TPE)	**Miss J.Novotna [5]** 6/2 6/1		......................6/4 6/3			
64. **Miss J.Novotna [5]** ....(CZE)		......................6/3 6/1				
65. **Miss N.Tauziat [8]** ....(FRA)	**Miss N.Tauziat [8]** 6/3 6/2					
(W) 66. Miss L.A.Ahl ....(GBR)		**Miss N.Tauziat [8]**				
67. Miss A.Hopmans ....(NED)	Miss A.Hopmans 6/4 6/2					
68. Miss S.Kleinova ....(CZE)		......................6/3 6/4				
69. Miss J.Nejedly ....(CAN)	Miss S.Noorlander 6/4 6/2		**Miss N.Tauziat [8]**			
(Q) 70. Miss S.Noorlander ....(NED)		Miss S.Noorlander				
71. Miss A.Huber ....(GER)	Miss J.Capriati 5/7 6/3 9/7		......................6/1 6/1			
72. Miss J.Capriati ....(USA)				Miss N.Tauziat [8]		
73. Miss M.Grzybowska ....(POL)	Miss A.Sugiyama 6/1 6/2			......................6/3 3/6 6/3		
74. Miss A.Sugiyama ....(JPN)		Miss E.Likhovtseva				
75. Miss A.Molik ....(AUS)	Miss E.Likhovtseva 6/2 6/0					
76. Miss E.Likhovtseva ....(RUS)		......................7/6(6) 6/3				
77. Miss K.Boogert ....(NED)	Miss K.Boogert 6/4 7/5		Mrs D.Van Roost [15]			
78. Miss C.Rubin ....(USA)		Mrs D.Van Roost [15]				
(L) 79. Miss E.Dementieva ....(RUS)	Mrs D.Van Roost [15] 3/6 6/4 6/4		......................6/4 7/6(4)			
80. **Mrs D.Van Roost [15]** ....(BEL)		......................6/3 6/2				
81. **Miss S.Testud [13]** ....(FRA)	**Miss S.Testud [13]** 6/1 6/3					
(W) 82. Miss J.M.Pullin ....(GBR)		**Miss S.Testud [13]**				
83. Miss D.Chladkova ....(CZE)	Miss B.Rittner 6/4 6/2					
84. Miss B.Rittner ....(GER)		......................7/6(2) 6/1				
85. Miss M.Drake ....(CAN)	Miss M.Drake 6/3 6/0		Miss T.Tanasugarn			
86. Miss E.Koulikovskaya ....(RUS)		Miss T.Tanasugarn				
87. Miss T.Tanasugarn ....(THA)	Miss T.Tanasugarn 6/1 6/4		......................6/2 1/6 6/3			
88. Miss K.Hrdlickova ....(CZE)		......................6/4 6/3		Miss M.Lucic		
89. Miss M.Diaz Oliva ....(ARG)	Miss M.Diaz Oliva ....7/6(3) 7/5			....................7/5 6/3		
90. Miss A.Smashnova ....(ISR)		Miss M.Lucic				
(Q) 91. Miss E.R.De Lone ....(USA)	Miss M.Lucic ....3/6 7/6(4) 7/5					
92. Miss M.Lucic ....(CRO)		......................6/2 6/1				
(W) 93. Miss J.Ward ....(GBR)	Miss M.Weingartner 4/6 7/5 6/3		Miss M.Lucic			
94. Miss M.Weingartner ....(GER)		**Miss M.Seles [4]**				
95. Miss C.Torrens-Valero ....(ESP)	**Miss M.Seles [4]** 6/3 6/1		......................7/6(4) 7/6(4)			
96. **Miss M.Seles [4]** ....(USA)		......................6/0 6/0				
97. **Miss V.Williams [6]** ....(USA)	**Miss V.Williams [6]** 6/1 7/5				Miss M.Lucic	
98. Miss M.Oremans ....(NED)		**Miss V.Williams [6]**			4/6 6/4 7/5	
99. Miss J.Chi ....(USA)	Miss E.Tatarkova 7/5 6/0					
100. Miss E.Tatarkova ....(UKR)		......................6/3 6/4				
101. Miss K.Srebotnik ....(SLO)	Miss S.Pitkowski ......7/6(5) 5/7 6/1		**Miss V.Williams [6]**			
102. Miss S.Pitkowski ....(FRA)		Miss S.Pitkowski				
103. Miss A-G.Sidot ....(FRA)	Miss L.Latimer 6/4 6/2		......................6/1 6/1			
(W)104. Miss L.Latimer ....(GBR)		......................7/5 5/7 6/3		Miss V.Williams [6]		
105. Miss R.Dragomir ....(ROM)	Miss R.Dragomir 7/5 6/3			......................3/6 6/3 6/2		
106. Miss P.Suarez ....(ARG)		Miss I.Gorrochategui				
107. Miss I.Gorrochategui ....(ARG)	Miss I.Gorrochategui 6/2 1/6 6/2					
108. Miss S.Smith ....(GBR)		......................6/2 6/2				
109. Miss M.A.Vento ....(VEN)	Miss M.A.Vento 7/5 6/3		**Miss A.Kournikova [17]**			
110. Miss E.Gagliardi ....(SUI)		**Miss A.Kournikova [17]**				
(W)111. Miss B.Schwartz ....(AUT)	**Miss A.Kournikova [17]** 7/6(2) 4/6 6/2		......................7/5 3/1 Ret'd			
112. **Miss A.Kournikova [17]** ......(RUS)		......................7/5 6/4				
113. **Miss A.J.Coetzer [12]** ....(RSA)	**Miss A.J.Coetzer [12]** 6/2 7/5					Miss S.Graf [2]
114. Miss N.J.Pratt ....(AUS)		**Miss A.J.Coetzer [12]**				6/4 7/5
115. Miss C.Papadaki ....(GRE)	Miss M.Saeki 6/3 6/2					
116. Miss M.Saeki ....(JPN)		......................6/4 6/1				
117. Miss J.Kruger ....(RSA)	Miss K.Clijsters 6/2 6/3		Miss K.Clijsters			
(Q)118. Miss K.Clijsters ....(BEL)		Miss K.Clijsters				
119. Miss L.Osterloh ....(USA)	Miss K.M.Cross 6/1 6/3		......................6/2 6/0			
(W)120. Miss K.M.Cross ....(GBR)				Miss K.Clijsters		
121. Miss K-A.Guse ....(AUS)	Miss J.Lee 3/6 6/4 6/1			......................6/2 6/4		
122. Miss J.Lee ....(TPE)		Miss C.Morariu				
123. Miss C.Morariu ....(USA)	Miss C.Morariu ....7/6(8) 3/6 6/2					
124. Miss L.Courtois ....(BEL)		......................6/2 6/4				
125. Miss J.Watanabe ....(USA)	Miss M.de Swardt 6/1 6/4		Miss S.Graf [2]		Miss S.Graf [2]	
126. Miss M.de Swardt ....(RSA)		**Miss S.Graf [2]**			6/7(3) 6/4 6/3	
127. Miss L.Cervanova ....(SVK)	**Miss S.Graf [2]** 6/1 6/4		......................6/1 6/3			
128. **Miss S.Graf [2]** ....(GER)		......................4/6 6/3 6/2				

Miss A.Stevenson 6/3 6/1

Miss L.A.Davenport [3] 6/3 6/4

Miss J.Novotna [5] 6/3 7/5

Miss N.Tauziat [8] 6/3 6/2

Miss M.Lucic 7/5 6/3

Miss S.Graf [2] 6/2 6/2

Miss L.A.Davenport [3] 6/2 6/3

Miss L.A.Davenport [3] 6/4 7/5

Miss S.Graf [2] 6/2 3/6 6/4

Holders: Miss M.Hingis and Miss J.Novotna

The winners become the holders, for the year only, of the CHALLENGE CUP presented by HRH PRINCESS MARINA, DUCHESS OF KENT, the late President of The All England Lawn Tennis and Croquet Club. The winners receive silver replicas of the Challenge Cup. A silver salver is presented to each of the runners-up and a bronze medal to each defeated semi-finalist.

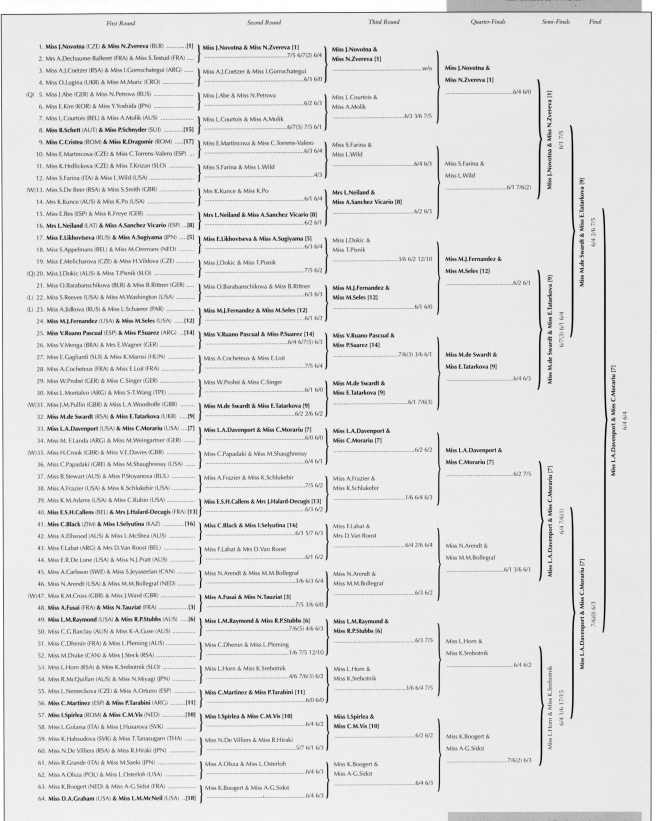

	First Round	Second Round	Third Round	Quarter-Finals	Semi-Finals	Final
1.	Miss J.Novotna (CZE) & Miss N.Zvereva (BLR) ......[1]	Miss J.Novotna & Miss N.Zvereva [1]				
2.	Mrs A.Dechaume-Balleret (FRA) & Miss S.Testud (FRA)	......7/5 6/7(2) 6/4	Miss J.Novotna & Miss N.Zvereva [1]			
3.	Miss A.J.Coetzer (RSA) & Miss I.Gorrochategui (ARG)	Miss A.J.Coetzer & Miss I.Gorrochategui		Miss J.Novotna & Miss N.Zvereva [1]		
4.	Miss O.Lugina (UKR) & Miss M.Muric (CRO)	......6/3 6/0	......w/o			
(Q) 5.	Miss J.Abe (GER) & Miss N.Petrova (RUS)	Miss J.Abe & Miss N.Petrova		......6/4 6/0		
6.	Miss E.Kim (KOR) & Miss Y.Yoshida (JPN)	......6/2 6/3	Miss L.Courtois & Miss A.Molik			
7.	Miss L.Courtois (BEL) & Miss A.Molik (AUS)	Miss L.Courtois & Miss A.Molik			Miss J.Novotna & Miss N.Zvereva [1]	
8.	Miss B.Schett (AUT) & Miss P.Schnyder (SUI) ....[15]	......6/7(5) 7/5 6/1	......6/3 3/6 7/5		6/1 7/5	
9.	Miss C.Cristea (ROM) & Miss R.Dragomir (ROM) ...[17]	Miss E.Martincova & Miss C.Torrens-Valero				
10.	Miss E.Martincova (CZE) & Miss C.Torrens-Valero (ESP) ...	......6/3 6/4	Miss S.Farina & Miss L.Wild			
11.	Miss K.Hrdlickova (CZE) & Miss T.Krizan (SLO)	Miss S.Farina & Miss L.Wild	......6/4 6/3	Miss S.Farina & Miss L.Wild		
12.	Miss S.Farina (ITA) & Miss L.Wild (USA)	......4/3				
(W)13.	Miss S.De Beer (RSA) & Miss S.Smith (GBR)	Mrs K.Kunce & Miss K.Po		......6/1 7/6(2)		
14.	Mrs K.Kunce (AUS) & Miss K.Po (USA)	......6/1 6/4	Mrs L.Neiland & Miss A.Sanchez Vicario [8]			
15.	Miss E.Bes (ESP) & Miss K.Freye (GER)	Mrs L.Neiland & Miss A.Sanchez Vicario [8]	......6/2 6/3			
16.	Mrs L.Neiland (LAT) & Miss A.Sanchez Vicario (ESP) ...[8]	......6/2 6/1				
17.	Miss E.Likhovtseva (RUS) & Miss A.Sugiyama (JPN) .....[5]	Miss E.Likhovtseva & Miss A.Sugiyama [5]				
18.	Miss S.Appelmans (BEL) & Miss M.Oremans (NED)	......6/3 6/4	Miss J.Dokic & Miss T.Pisnik			
19.	Miss E.Melicharova (CZE) & Miss H.Vildova (CZE)	Miss J.Dokic & Miss T.Pisnik	......3/6 6/2 12/10	Miss M.J.Fernandez & Miss M.Seles [12]		
(Q) 20.	Miss J.Dokic (AUS) & Miss T.Pisnik (SLO)	......7/5 6/2				
21.	Miss O.Barabanschikova (BLR) & Miss B.Rittner (GER)	Miss O.Barabanschikova & Miss B.Rittner		......6/2 6/1		
(L) 22.	Miss S.Reeves (USA) & Miss M.Washington (USA)	......6/3 6/3	Miss M.J.Fernandez & Miss M.Seles [12]			
(L) 23.	Miss A.Jidkova (RUS) & Miss L.Schaerer (PAR)	Miss M.J.Fernandez & Miss M.Seles [12]	......6/1 6/0		Miss M.de Swardt & Miss E.Tatarkova [9]	
24.	Miss M.J.Fernandez (USA) & Miss M.Seles (USA) ......[12]	......6/1 6/2			6/4 2/6 7/5	
25.	Miss V.Ruano Pascual (ESP) & Miss P.Suarez (ARG) .....[14]	Miss V.Ruano Pascual & Miss P.Suarez [14]				
26.	Miss V.Menga (BRA) & Mrs E.Wagner (GER)	......6/4 6/7(5) 6/3	Miss V.Ruano Pascual & Miss P.Suarez [14]			
27.	Miss E.Gagliardi (SUI) & Miss K.Marosi (HUN)	Miss A.Cocheteux & Miss E.Loit	......7/6(3) 3/6 6/1	Miss M.de Swardt & Miss E.Tatarkova [9]		
28.	Miss A.Cocheteux (FRA) & Miss E.Loit (FRA)	......7/5 6/4				
29.	Miss W.Probst (GER) & Miss C.Singer (GER)	Miss W.Probst & Miss C.Singer		......6/4 6/3		
30.	Miss L.Montalvo (ARG) & Miss S-T.Wang (TPE)	......6/1 6/0	Miss M.de Swardt & Miss E.Tatarkova [9]			
(W)31.	Miss J.M.Pullin (GBR) & Miss L.A.Woodroffe (GBR)	Miss M.de Swardt & Miss E.Tatarkova [9]	......6/1 7/6(3)			
32.	Miss M.de Swardt (RSA) & Miss E.Tatarkova (UKR) ......[9]	......6/2 2/6 6/2				
33.	Miss L.A.Davenport (USA) & Miss C.Morariu (USA) ......[7]	Miss L.A.Davenport & Miss C.Morariu [7]				
34.	Miss M. F.Landa (ARG) & Miss M.Weingartner (GER)	......6/0 6/0	Miss L.A.Davenport & Miss C.Morariu [7]			
(W)35.	Miss H.Crook (GBR) & Miss V.E.Davies (GBR)	Miss C.Papadaki & Miss M.Shaughnessy	......6/2 6/2	Miss L.A.Davenport & Miss C.Morariu [7]		
36.	Miss C.Papadaki (GRE) & Miss M.Shaughnessy (USA)	......6/4 6/1				
37.	Miss B.Stewart (AUS) & Miss P.Stoyanova (BUL)	Miss A.Frazier & Miss K.Schlukebir		......6/2 7/5		
38.	Miss A.Frazier (USA) & Miss K.Schlukebir (USA)	......7/5 6/2	Miss A.Frazier & Miss K.Schlukebir			
39.	Miss K.M.Adams (USA) & Miss C.Rubin (USA)	Miss E.S.H.Callens & Mrs J.Halard-Decugis [13]	......1/6 6/4 6/3		Miss L.A.Davenport & Miss C.Morariu [7]	
40.	Miss E.S.H.Callens (BEL) & Mrs J.Halard-Decugis (FRA) [13]	......6/3 6/2			6/4 7/6(1)	
41.	Miss C.Black (ZIM) & Miss I.Selyutina (KAZ) ....[16]	Miss C.Black & Miss I.Selyutina [16]				
42.	Miss A.Ellwood (AUS) & Miss L.McShea (AUS)	......6/3 5/7 6/3	Miss F.Labat & Mrs D.Van Roost			
43.	Miss F.Labat (ARG) & Mrs D.Van Roost (BEL)	Miss F.Labat & Mrs D.Van Roost	......6/4 2/6 6/4	Miss N.Arendt & Miss M.M.Bollegraf		
44.	Miss E.R.De Lone (USA) & Miss N.J.Pratt (AUS)	......6/1 6/2				
45.	Miss A.Carlsson (SWE) & Miss S.Jeyaseelan (CAN)	Miss N.Arendt & Miss M.M.Bollegraf		......6/1 3/6 6/1		
46.	Miss N.Arendt (USA) & Miss M.M.Bollegraf (NED)	......3/6 6/3 6/4	Miss N.Arendt & Miss M.M.Bollegraf			
(W)47.	Miss K.M.Cross (GBR) & Miss J.Ward (GBR)	Miss A.Fusai & Miss N.Tauziat [3]	......6/3 6/2			
48.	Miss A.Fusai (FRA) & Miss N.Tauziat (FRA) ....[3]	......7/5 3/6 6/0				
49.	Miss L.M.Raymond (USA) & Miss R.P.Stubbs (AUS) ......[6]	Miss L.M.Raymond & Miss R.P.Stubbs [6]			Miss L.A.Davenport & Miss C.Morariu [7]	
50.	Miss C.G.Barclay (AUS) & Miss K-A.Guse (AUS)	......7/6(5) 4/6 6/3	Miss L.M.Raymond & Miss R.P.Stubbs [6]		7/6(0) 6/3	
51.	Miss C.Dhenin (FRA) & Miss L.Pleming (AUS)	Miss C.Dhenin & Miss L.Pleming	......6/3 7/5	Miss L.Horn & Miss K.Srebotnik		
52.	Miss M.Drake (CAN) & Miss J.Steck (RSA)	......1/6 7/5 12/10				
53.	Miss L.Horn (RSA) & Miss K.Srebotnik (SLO)	Miss L.Horn & Miss K.Srebotnik		......6/4 6/2		
54.	Miss R.McQuillan (AUS) & Miss N.Miyagi (JPN)	......4/6 7/6(3) 6/2	Miss L.Horn & Miss K.Srebotnik			
55.	Miss L.Nemeckova (CZE) & Miss A.Ortuno (ESP)	Miss C.Martinez & Miss P.Tarabini [11]	......3/6 6/4 7/5		Miss L.Horn & Miss K.Srebotnik	
56.	Miss C.Martinez (ESP) & Miss P.Tarabini (ARG) ......[11]	......6/0 6/0			6/4 1/6 17/15	
57.	Miss I.Spirlea (ROM) & Miss C.M.Vis (NED) ....[10]	Miss I.Spirlea & Miss C.M.Vis [10]				
58.	Miss L.Golarsa (ITA) & Miss J.Husarova (SVK)	......6/4 6/2	Miss I.Spirlea & Miss C.M.Vis [10]			
59.	Miss K.Habsudova (SVK) & Miss T.Tanasugarn (THA)	Miss N.De Villiers & Miss R.Hiraki	......6/2 6/2	Miss K.Boogert & Miss A-G.Sidot		
60.	Miss N.De Villiers (RSA) & Miss R.Hiraki (JPN)	......5/7 6/1 6/3				
61.	Miss R.Grande (ITA) & Miss M.Saeki (JPN)	Miss A.Olsza & Miss L.Osterloh		......7/6(2) 6/3		
62.	Miss A.Olsza (POL) & Miss L.Osterloh (USA)	......6/4 6/3	Miss K.Boogert & Miss A-G.Sidot			
63.	Miss K.Boogert (NED) & Miss A-G.Sidot (FRA)	Miss K.Boogert & Miss A-G.Sidot	......6/4 6/3			
64.	Miss D.A.Graham (USA) & Miss L.M.McNeil (USA) ..[18]	......6/4 6/3				

Final: Miss L.A.Davenport & Miss C.Morariu [7] def. Miss M.de Swardt & Miss E.Tatarkova [9] 6/4 6/4

Heavy type denotes seeded players. The figure in brackets against names denotes the order in which they have been seeded.
(W) = Wild card. (Q) = Qualifier. (L) = Lucky loser.

The matches are the best of three sets

The winners become the holders, for the year only, of the CHALLENGE CUP presented by the family of the late Mr S.H. SMITH. The winners receive silver replicas of the Challenge Cup. A silver salver is presented to each of the runners-up and a bronze medal to each defeated semi-finalist.

Holders: M.Mirnyi and Miss S.Williams

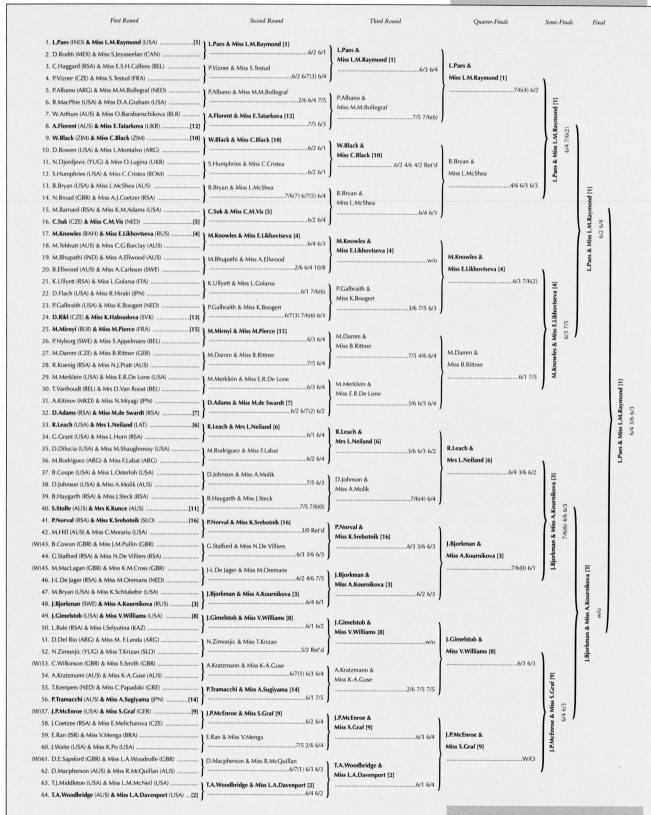

First Round	Second Round	Third Round	Quarter-Finals	Semi-Finals	Final
1. L.Paes (IND) & Miss L.M.Raymond (USA) ...[1]	L.Paes & Miss L.M.Raymond [1]				
2. D.Roditi (MEX) & Miss S.Jeyaseelan (CAN)	6/2 6/1	L.Paes & Miss L.M.Raymond [1]			
3. C.Haggard (RSA) & Miss E.S.H.Callens (BEL)	P.Vizner & Miss S.Testud	6/3 6/4	L.Paes & Miss L.M.Raymond [1]		
4. P.Vizner (CZE) & Miss S.Testud (FRA)	6/2 6/7(3) 6/4				
5. P.Albano (ARG) & Miss M.M.Bollegraf (NED)	P.Albano & Miss M.M.Bollegraf		7/6(4) 6/2		
6. B.MacPhie (USA) & Miss D.A.Graham (USA)	2/6 6/4 7/5	P.Albano & Miss M.M.Bollegraf			
7. W.Arthurs (AUS) & Miss O.Barabanschikova (BLR)	A.Florent & Miss E.Tatarkova [12]	7/5 7/6(6)			
8. A.Florent (AUS) & Miss E.Tatarkova (UKR) ...[12]	7/5 6/3			L.Paes & Miss L.M.Raymond [1] 6/4 7/6(2)	
9. W.Black (ZIM) & C.Black (ZIM) ...[10]	W.Black & Miss C.Black [10]				
10. D.Bowen (USA) & Miss L.Montalvo (ARG)	6/2 6/1	W.Black & Miss C.Black [10]			
11. N.Djordjevic (YUG) & Miss O.Lugina (UKR)	S.Humphries & Miss C.Cristea	6/2 4/6 4/2 Ret'd	B.Bryan & Miss L.McShea		
12. S.Humphries (USA) & Miss C.Cristea (ROM)	6/2 6/1				
13. B.Bryan (USA) & Miss L.McShea (AUS)	B.Bryan & Miss L.McShea		4/6 6/3 6/3		
14. N.Broad (GBR) & Miss A.J.Coetzer (RSA)	7/6(7) 6/7(5) 6/4	B.Bryan & Miss L.McShea			L.Paes & Miss L.M.Raymond [1] 6/2 6/4
15. M.Barnard (RSA) & Miss K.M.Adams (USA)	C.Suk & Miss C.M.Vis [5]	6/4 6/3			
16. C.Suk (CZE) & Miss C.M.Vis (NED) ...[5]	6/2 6/4				
17. M.Knowles (BAH) & Miss E.Likhovtseva (RUS) ...[4]	M.Knowles & Miss E.Likhovtseva [4]				
18. M.Tebbutt (AUS) & Miss C.G.Barclay (AUS)	6/4 6/3	M.Knowles & Miss E.Likhovtseva [4]			
19. M.Bhupathi (IND) & Miss A.Ellwood (AUS)	M.Bhupathi & Miss A.Ellwood	w/o	M.Knowles & Miss E.Likhovtseva [4]		
20. B.Ellwood (AUS) & Miss A.Carlsson (SWE)	2/6 6/4 10/8		6/3 7/6(2)		
21. K.Ullyett (RSA) & Miss L.Golarsa (ITA)	K.Ullyett & Miss L.Golarsa				
22. D.Flach (USA) & Miss R.Hiraki (JPN)	6/1 7/6(6)	P.Galbraith & Miss K.Boogert			
23. P.Galbraith (USA) & Miss K.Boogert (NED)	P.Galbraith & Miss K.Boogert	3/6 7/5 6/3		M.Knowles & Miss E.Likhovtseva [4] 6/3 7/5	
24. D.Rikl (CZE) & Miss K.Habsudova (SVK) ...[13]	6/7(3) 7/6(6) 6/3				
25. M.Mirnyi (BLR) & Miss M.Pierce (FRA) ...[15]	M.Mirnyi & Miss M.Pierce [15]				
26. P.Nyborg (SWE) & Miss S.Appelmans (BEL)	6/3 6/4	M.Damm & Miss B.Rittner			
27. M.Damm (CZE) & Miss B.Rittner (GER)	M.Damm & Miss B.Rittner	7/5 4/6 6/4	M.Damm & Miss B.Rittner		
28. R.Koenig (RSA) & Miss N.J.Pratt (AUS)	7/5 6/4		6/1 7/5		
29. M.Merklein (USA) & Miss E.R.De Lone (USA)	M.Merklein & Miss E.R.De Lone				
30. T.Vanhoudt (BEL) & Mrs D.Van Roost (BEL)	6/3 6/4	M.Merklein & Miss E.R.De Lone			
31. A.Kitinov (MKD) & Miss N.Miyagi (JPN)	D.Adams & Miss M.de Swardt [7]	3/6 6/3 6/4			
32. D.Adams (RSA) & Miss M.de Swardt (RSA) ...[7]	6/2 6/7(2) 6/2			L.Paes & Miss L.M.Raymond [1] 6/4 3/6 6/3	
33. R.Leach (USA) & Mrs L.Neiland (LAT) ...[6]	R.Leach & Mrs L.Neiland [6]				
34. G.Grant (USA) & Miss L.Horn (RSA)	6/1 6/4	R.Leach & Mrs L.Neiland [6]			
35. D.Dilucia (USA) & Miss M.Shaughnessy (USA)	M.Rodriguez & Miss F.Labat	3/6 6/3 6/2	R.Leach & Mrs L.Neiland [6]		
36. M.Rodriguez (ARG) & Miss F.Labat (ARG)	6/2 6/4		6/4 3/6 6/2		
37. B.Coupe (USA) & Miss L.Osterloh (USA)	D.Johnson & Miss A.Molik				
38. D.Johnson (USA) & Miss A.Molik (AUS)	7/5 6/3	D.Johnson & Miss A.Molik			
39. B.Haygarth (RSA) & Miss J.Steck (RSA)	B.Haygarth & Miss J.Steck	7/6(4) 6/4			
40. S.Stolle (AUS) & Mrs K.Kunce (AUS) ...[11]	7/5 7/6(0)			J.Bjorkman & Miss A.Kournikova [3] 7/6(6) 4/6 6/3	
41. P.Norval (RSA) & Miss K.Srebotnik (SLO) ...[16]	P.Norval & Miss K.Srebotnik [16]				
42. M.Hill (AUS) & Miss C.Morariu (USA)	3/0 Ret'd	P.Norval & Miss K.Srebotnik [16]			
(W)43. B.Cowan (GBR) & Miss J.M.Pullin (GBR)	G.Stafford & Miss N.De Villiers	6/3 3/6 6/3	J.Bjorkman & Miss A.Kournikova [3]		
44. G.Stafford (RSA) & Miss N.De Villiers (RSA)	6/3 3/6 6/3		7/6(0) 6/1		
(W)45. M.MacLagan (GBR) & Miss K.M.Cross (GBR)	J-L.De Jager & Miss M.Oremans				
46. J-L.De Jager (RSA) & Miss M.Oremans (NED)	6/2 4/6 7/5	J.Bjorkman & Miss A.Kournikova [3]			
47. M.Bryan (USA) & Miss K.Schlukebir (USA)	J.Bjorkman & Miss A.Kournikova [3]	6/2 6/3			
48. J.Bjorkman (SWE) & Miss A.Kournikova (RUS) ...[3]	6/4 6/1			J.Bjorkman & Miss A.Kournikova [3] w/o	
49. J.Gimelstob (USA) & Miss V.Williams (USA) ...[8]	J.Gimelstob & Miss V.Williams [8]				
50. L.Bale (RSA) & Miss I.Selyutina (KAZ)	6/1 6/2	J.Gimelstob & Miss V.Williams [8]			
51. D.Del Rio (ARG) & Miss M.F.Landa (ARG)	N.Zimonjic & Miss T.Krizan	w/o	J.Gimelstob & Miss V.Williams [8]		
52. N.Zimonjic (YUG) & Miss T.Krizan (SLO)	5/2 Ret'd		6/3 6/3		
(W)53. C.Wilkinson (GBR) & Miss S.Smith (GBR)	A.Kratzmann & Miss K-A.Guse				
54. A.Kratzmann (AUS) & Miss K-A.Guse (AUS)	6/7(1) 6/3 6/4	A.Kratzmann & Miss K-A.Guse			
55. T.Kempers (NED) & Miss C.Papadaki (GRE)	P.Tramacchi & Miss A.Sugiyama [14]	2/6 7/5 7/5			J.P.McEnroe & Miss S.Graf [9] 6/4 6/3
56. P.Tramacchi (AUS) & Miss A.Sugiyama (JPN) ...[14]	6/1 7/5				
(W)57. J.P.McEnroe (USA) & Miss S.Graf (GER) ...[9]	J.P.McEnroe & Miss S.Graf [9]				
58. J.Coetzee (RSA) & Miss E.Melicharova (CZE)	6/2 6/4	J.P.McEnroe & Miss S.Graf [9]			
59. E.Ran (ISR) & Miss V.Menga (BRA)	E.Ran & Miss V.Menga	6/3 6/4	J.P.McEnroe & Miss S.Graf [9]		
60. J.Waite (USA) & Miss K.Po (USA)	7/5 2/6 6/4		W/O		
(W)61. D.E.Sapsford (GBR) & Miss L.A.Woodroffe (GBR)	D.Macpherson & Miss R.McQuillan				
62. D.Macpherson (AUS) & Miss R.McQuillan (AUS)	6/7(1) 6/3 6/2	T.A.Woodbridge & Miss L.A.Davenport [2]			
63. T.J.Middleton (USA) & Miss L.M.McNeil (USA)	T.A.Woodbridge & Miss L.A.Davenport [2]	6/1 6/4			
64. T.A.Woodbridge (AUS) & Miss L.A.Davenport (USA) ...[2]	6/4 6/2				

Heavy type denotes seeded players. The figure in brackets against names denotes the order in which they have been seeded. (W) = Wild card. (Q) = Qualifier. (L) = Lucky loser.

The matches are the best of three sets

The winners become the holders, for the year only, of a Cup presented by The All England Lawn Tennis and Croquet Club. The winners receive miniature silver salvers. A silver medal is presented to each of the runners-up.

Holders: G.Mayer and T.Wilkison

	v				WINS	LOSSES	SEMI-FINAL	FINAL
GROUP A								
M.J. Bates (GBR) and R. Krishnan (IND)	v	M.R. Edmondson and P. Fleming 6/7(5) 6/7(8)	M. Pernfors and S. Zivojinovic 6/4 3/6 6/1	J.B. Fitzgerald and W. Masur 6/4 6/7(5) 4/6	1	2		
M.R. Edmondson (AUS) and P. Fleming (USA)	v	**M.J. Bates and R. Krishnan** 7/6(5) 7/6(8)	J.B. Fitzgerald and W. Masur 3/6 6/4 5/7	M. Pernfors and S. Zivojinovic 6/2 6/2	2	1		
J.B. Fitzgerald (AUS) and W. Masur (AUS)	v	M. Pernfors and S. Zivojinovic 6/2 6/3	M.R. Edmondson and P. Fleming 6/3 4/6 7/5	**M.J. Bates and R. Krishnan** 4/6 7/6(5) 6/4	3	0	J.B. Fitzgerald and W. Masur	
M. Pernfors (SWE) and S. Zivojinovic (YUG)	v	J.B. Fitzgerald and W. Masur 2/6 3/6	**M.J. Bates and R. Krishnan** 4/6 6/3 1/6	M.R. Edmondson and P. Fleming 2/6 2/6	0	3		
GROUP B								
G.W. Donnelly (USA) and D. Visser (RSA)	v	C. Dowdeswell and C.J. Mottram 6/7(5) 3/6	P.B. McNamara and P.F. McNamee 3/6 6/7(5)	H. Guenthardt and B. Taroczy 6/1 6/4	1	2		
C. Dowdeswell (GBR) and C.J. Mottram (GBR)	v	**G.W. Donnelly and D. Visser** 7/6(5) 6/3	H. Guenthardt and B. Taroczy 7/5 6/3	P.B. McNamara and P.F. McNamee 3/6 6/7(3)	2	1		
H. Guenthardt (SUI) and B. Taroczy (HUN)	v	P.B. McNamara and P.F. McNamee 5/7 7/6(5) 3/6	C. Dowdeswell and C.J. Mottram 5/7 6/3	**G.W. Donnelly and D. Visser** 1/6 4/6	0	3	P.B. McNamara and P.F. McNamee	P.B. McNamara and P.F. McNamee 6/7(1) 7/6(6) 6/3
P.B. McNamara (AUS) and P.F. McNamee (AUS)	v	H. Guenthardt and B. Taroczy 7/5 6/7(5) 6/3	**G.W. Donnelly and D. Visser** 6/3 7/6(5)	C. Dowdeswell and C.J. Mottram 6/3 7/6(3)	3	0		
GROUP C								
G. Mayer (USA) and T. Wilkison (USA)	v	P. Slozil and T. Smid 6/4 6/7(5) 7/5	P. Dupre and C.J. Van Rensburg 6/4 7/5	A. Jarryd and J. Nystrom 4/6 4/6	2	1		
P. Dupre (USA) and C.J. Van Rensburg (RSA)	v	A. Jarryd and J. Nystrom 3/6 3/6	**G. Mayer and T. Wilkison** 4/6 5/7	P. Slozil and T. Smid 4/6 6/7(5)	0	3		
A. Jarryd (SWE) and J. Nystrom (SWE)	v	P. Dupre and C.J. Van Rensburg 6/3 6/3	P. Slozil and T. Smid 6/1 6/3	**G. Mayer and T. Wilkison** 6/4 6/4	3	0	A. Jarryd and J. Nystrom	
P. Slozil (CZE) and T. Smid (CZE)	v	**G. Mayer and T. Wilkison** 4/6 7/6(5) 5/7	A. Jarryd and J. Nystrom 1/6 3/6	P. Dupre and C.J. Van Rensburg 6/4 7/6(5)	1	2		K. Flach and R. Seguso 6/3 3/6 9/7
GROUP D								
K. Curren (USA) and J. Kriek (USA)	v	M. Bahrami and H. Leconte 7/5 6/7(5) 10/8	J. Grabb and J. Pugh 4/6 4/6	K. Flach and R. Seguso 6/3 3/6 9/8(3)	2	1		
M. Bahrami (IRI) and H. Leconte (FRA)	v	**K. Curren and J. Kriek** 5/7 7/6(5) 8/10	K. Flach and R. Seguso 4/6 0/6	J. Grabb and J. Pugh 2/6 4/6	0	3	K. Flach and R. Seguso	K. Flach and R. Seguso 4/6 7/6(3) 6/4
K. Flach (USA) and R. Seguso (USA)	v	J. Grabb and J. Pugh 7/6(4) 6/3	M. Bahrami and H. Leconte 6/4 6/0	**K. Curren and J. Kriek** 3/6 6/3 8/9(3)	2	1		
J. Grabb (USA) and J. Pugh (USA)	v	K. Flach and R. Seguso 6/7(4) 3/6	**K. Curren and J. Kriek** 6/4 6/4	M. Bahrami and H. Leconte 6/2 6/4	2	1		

This event is played on a 'round robin' basis. Sixteen invited pairs are divided into four groups and each pair in each group plays the others. The pairs winning most matches are the winners of their respective groups and play semi-final and final rounds as indicated above. If matches should be equal in any group, the head-to-head result between the two pairs with the same number of wins determines the winning pair of the group. Heavy type denotes seeded players. **The matches are the best of three sets**

THE 45 AND OVER GENTLEMEN'S INVITATION DOUBLES

The winners become the holders, for the year only, of a Cup presented by The All England Lawn Tennis and Croquet Club. The winners receive miniature silver salvers. A silver medal is presented to each of the runners-up.

Holders: M.C.Riessen and S.E.Stewart

First Round	Second Round	Semi-Finals	Final
1. **M.C.Riessen (USA) & S.E.Stewart (USA)** ....[1]	I.Nastase & T.S.Okker		
2. I.Nastase (ROM) & T.S.Okker (NED) .... 7/6(8) 6/7(6) 6/1		I.Nastase & T.S.Okker	
3. J.G.Alexander (AUS) & R.Drysdale (GBR)	J.G.Alexander & R.Drysdale		
4. A.A.Mayer (USA) & R.Tanner (USA) 6/4 7/5			7/6(5) 7/5
5. **O.K.Davidson (AUS) & E.C.Drysdale (RSA)** ......[3]	R.L.Case & G.Masters		
6. R.L.Case (AUS) & G.Masters (AUS) 6/3 6/1		R.L.Case & G.Masters	
7. R.J.Frawley (AUS) & A.Metreveli (RUS)	R.J.Frawley & A.Metreveli		
8. M.Cox (GBR) & M.Santana (ESP) 6/2 6/4		6/2 6/2	R.L.Case & G.Masters
9. J.D.Newcombe (AUS) & A.D.Roche (AUS)	J.D.Newcombe & A.D.Roche		6/4 6/7(5) 6/3
10. F.D.McMillan (RSA) & A.Stone (AUS) 6/4 6/3		J.Fillol & R.L.Stockton [4]	
11. K.R.Rosewall (AUS) & F.S.Stolle (AUS)	**J.Fillol & R.L.Stockton [4]**		
12. **J.Fillol (CHI) & R.L.Stockton (USA)** ....[4]	6/2 6/3	6/3 6/4	B.E.Gottfried & T.R.Gullikson [2]
13. R.C.Lutz (USA) & S.R.Smith (USA)	R.C.Lutz & S.R.Smith		6/2 4/6 6/4
14. J.W.Feaver (GBR) & R.Taylor (GBR) 6/4 6/2		B.E.Gottfried & T.R.Gullikson [2]	
15. A.Amritraj (IND) & V.Amritraj (IND)	**B.E.Gottfried & T.R.Gullikson [2]**		
16. **B.E.Gottfried (USA) & T.R.Gullikson (USA)** ....[2]	6/1 3/6 11/9	6/3 6/4	

Winner: B.E.Gottfried & T.R.Gullikson [2] 6/1 7/6(0)

Heavy type denotes seeded players. The figure in brackets against names denotes the order in which they have been seeded.
The matches are the best of three sets

The winners become the holders, for the year only, of a Cup presented by The All England Lawn Tennis and Croquet Club. The winners receive miniature Cups. A silver medal is presented to each of the runners-up.

Holders: Miss P.H.Shriver and Miss P.D.Smylie

GROUP A				WINS	LOSSES	FINAL
Miss G. Fernandez (USA) and Miss Y. Vermaak (RSA) v	Mrs G. Magers and Miss B.F. Stove 3/6 6/3 5/7	Miss R. Casals and Miss A. Hobbs 6/1 1/6 5/7	Miss H. Mandlikova and Miss S.V. Wade 6/2 3/0 Ret'd	1	2	
Mrs G. Magers (USA) and Miss B.F. Stove (NED) v	**Miss G. Fernandez and Miss Y. Vermaak** 6/3 3/6 7/5	Miss H. Mandlikova and Miss S.V. Wade 6/1 6/1	Miss R. Casals and Miss A. Hobbs 6/4 7/5	3	0	Mrs G. Magers and Miss B.F. Stove
Miss R. Casals (USA) and Miss A. Hobbs (GBR) v	Miss H. Mandlikova and Miss S.V. Wade 7/5 6/4	**Miss G. Fernandez and Miss Y. Vermaak** 1/6 6/1 7/5	Mrs G. Magers and Miss B.F. Stove 4/6 5/7	2	1	
Miss H. Mandlikova (AUS) and Miss S.V. Wade (GBR) v	Miss R. Casals and Miss A. Hobbs 5/7 4/6	Mrs G. Magers and Miss B.F. Stove 1/6 1/6	**Miss G. Fernandez and Miss Y. Vermaak** 2/6 0/3 Ret'd	0	3	
GROUP B						
Mrs P.D. Smylie (AUS) and Miss W.M. Turnbull (AUS) v	Miss B. Nagelsen and Mrs R. Nideffer 6/4 6/4	Miss J.M. Durie and Miss J.C. Russell 7/5 6/3	Miss M. Jausovec and Miss C. Kohde-Kilsch 6/2 6/3	3	0	Mrs P.D. Smylie and Miss W.M. Turnbull
Miss B. Nagelsen (USA) and Mrs R. Nideffer (RSA) v	**Mrs P.D. Smylie and Miss W.M. Turnbull** 4/6 4/6	Miss M. Jausovec and Miss C. Kohde-Kilsch 6/3 4/6 6/4	Miss J.M. Durie and Miss J.C. Russell 2/6 6/7(5)	1	2	
Miss J.M. Durie (GBR) and Miss J.C. Russell (USA) v	Miss M. Jausovec and Miss C. Kohde-Kilsch 7/6(3) 2/6 7/9	**Mrs P.D. Smylie and Miss W.M. Turnbull** 5/7 3/6	Miss B. Nagelsen and Mrs R. Nideffer 6/2 7/6(5)	1	2	
Miss M. Jausovec (SLO) and Miss C. Kohde-Kilsch (GER) v	Miss J.M. Durie and Miss J.C. Russell 6/7(3) 6/2 9/7	Miss B. Nagelsen and Mrs R. Nideffer 3/6 6/4 4/6	**Mrs P.D. Smylie and Miss W.M. Turnbull** 2/6 3/6	1	2	

FINAL: Mrs P.D. Smylie and Miss W.M. Turnbull 7/5 6/3

This event is played on a 'round robin' basis. Eight invited pairs are divided into two groups and each pair in each group plays the others. The pairs winning most matches are the winners of their respective groups and play a final round as indicated above. If matches should be equal in any group, the head-to-head result between the two pairs with the same number of wins determines the winning pair of the group.

Heavy type denotes seeded players.
The matches are the best of three sets

ALPHABETICAL LIST – 35 & OVER EVENTS

GENTLEMEN

Bahrami M. *(Iran)*
Bates M.J. *(Great Britain)*
Curren K. *(USA)*
Donnelly G.W. *(USA)*
Dowdeswell C. *(Great Britain)*
Dupre P. *(USA)*
Edmondson M.R. *(Australia)*
Fitzgerald J.B. *(Australia)*

Flach K. *(USA)*
Fleming P. *(USA)*
Grabb J. *(USA)*
Guenthardt H. *(Switzerland)*
Jarryd A. *(Sweden)*
Kriek J. *(USA)*
Krishnan R. *(India)*
Leconte H. *(France)*

Masur W. *(Australia)*
Mayer G. *(USA)*
McNamara P.B. *(Australia)*
McNamee P.F. *(Australia)*
Mottram C.J. *(Great Britain)*
Nystrom J. *(Sweden)*
Pernfors M. *(Sweden)*
Pugh J. *(USA)*

Seguso R. *(USA)*
Slozil P. *(Czech Republic)*
Smid T. *(Czech Republic)*
Taroczy B. *(Hungary)*
Van Rensburg C.J. *(South Africa)*
Visser D. *(South Africa)*
Wilkison T. *(USA)*
Zivojinovic S. *(Yugoslavia)*

LADIES

Casals Miss R. *(USA)*
Durie Miss J.M. *(Great Britain)*
Fernandez Miss G. *(USA)*
Hobbs Miss A. *(Great Britain)*

Jausovec Miss M. *(Slovenia)*
Kohde-Kilsch Miss C. *(Germany)*
Magers Mrs G. *(USA)*
Mandlikova Miss H. *(Australia)*

Nagelsen Miss B. *(USA)*
Nideffer Mrs R. *(South Africa)*
Russell Miss J.C. *(USA)*
Smylie Mrs P.D. *(Australia)*

Stove Miss B.F. *(Netherlands)*
Turnbull Miss W.M. *(Australia)*
Vermaak Miss Y. *(South Africa)*
Wade Miss S.V. *(Great Britain)*

ALPHABETICAL LIST – 45 & OVER EVENT

GENTLEMEN

Alexander J.G. *(Australia)*
Amritraj A. *(India)*
Amritraj V. *(India)*
Case R.L. *(Australia)*
Cox M. *(Great Britain)*
Davidson O.K. *(Australia)*
Drysdale E.C. *(South Africa)*
Drysdale R. *(Great Britain)*

Feaver J.W. *(Great Britain)*
Fillol J. *(Chile)*
Frawley R.J. *(Australia)*
Gottfried B.E. *(USA)*
Gullikson T.R. *(USA)*
Hewitt R.A.J. *(South Africa)*
Lutz R.C. *(USA)*
Masters G. *(Australia)*

Mayer A.A. *(USA)*
McMillan F.D. *(South Africa)*
Metreveli A. *(Russia)*
Nastase I. *(Romania)*
Newcombe J.D. *(Australia)*
Okker T.S. *(Netherlands)*
Riessen M.C. *(USA)*
Roche A.D. *(Australia)*

Rosewall K.R. *(Australia)*
Santana M. *(Spain)*
Smith S.R. *(USA)*
Stewart S.E. *(USA)*
Stockton R.L. *(USA)*
Stolle F.S. *(Australia)*
Tanner R. *(USA)*
Taylor R. *(Great Britain)*

For both the Boys' Singles *and* the Boys' Doubles Championships, the winners become the holders, for the year only, of a Cup presented by The All England Lawn Tennis and Croquet Club. The winners each receive a miniature Cup and the runners-up receive mementoes.

Holder: R.Federer

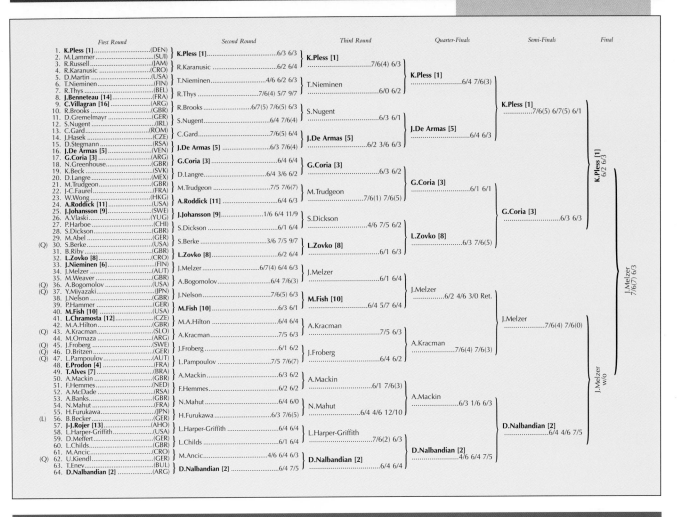

	First Round		Second Round	Third Round	Quarter-Finals	Semi-Finals	Final
1.	K.Pless [1] ....(DEN)	K.Pless [1] 6/3 6/3					
2.	M.Lammer ....(SUI)		K.Pless [1]				
3.	R.Russell ....(JAM)	R.Karanusic 6/2 6/4	.........................7/6(4) 6/3				
4.	R.Karanusic ....(CRO)			K.Pless [1]			
5.	D.Martin ....(USA)	T.Nieminen 4/6 6/2 6/3					
6.	T.Nieminen ....(FIN)		T.Nieminen				
7.	R.Thys ....(BEL)	R.Thys ....7/6(4) 5/7 9/7	.................................6/0 6/2				
8.	J.Benneteau [14] ....(FRA)				K.Pless [1]		
9.	C.Villagran [16] ....(ARG)	R.Brooks ....6/7(5) 7/6(5) 6/3			.........................6/4 7/6(3)		
10.	R.Brooks ....(GBR)		S.Nugent				
11.	D.Gremelmayr ....(GER)	S.Nugent ....6/4 7/6(4)	.................................6/3 6/1				
12.	S.Nugent ....(IRL)			J.De Armas [5]			
13.	C.Gard ....(ROM)	C.Gard ....7/6(5) 6/4		.........................6/4 6/3			
14.	J.Hasek ....(CZE)		J.De Armas [5]				
15.	D.Stegmann ....(RSA)	J.De Armas [5] ....6/3 7/6(4)	.............................6/2 3/6 6/3				
16.	J.De Armas [5] ....(VEN)					K.Pless [1]	
17.	G.Coria [3] ....(ARG)	G.Coria [3] 6/4 6/4				........7/6(5) 6/7(5) 6/1	
18.	N.Greenhouse ....(GBR)		G.Coria [3]				
19.	K.Beck ....(SVK)	D.Langre 6/4 3/6 6/2	.................................6/3 6/2				
20.	D.Langre ....(MEX)			G.Coria [3]			
21.	M.Trudgeon ....(GBR)	M.Trudgeon ....7/5 7/6(7)		.........................6/1 6/1			
22.	J-C.Faurel ....(FRA)		M.Trudgeon				
23.	W.Wong ....(HKG)	A.Roddick [11] 6/4 6/3	.......................7/6(1) 7/6(5)				
24.	A.Roddick [11] ....(USA)				G.Coria [3]		
25.	J.Johansson [9] ....(SWE)	J.Johansson [9] 1/6 6/4 11/9			.........................6/3 6/3		
26.	A.Vlaski ....(YUG)		S.Dickson				
27.	P.Harboe ....(CHI)	S.Dickson 6/1 6/4	.............................4/6 7/5 6/2				
28.	S.Dickson ....(GBR)			L.Zovko [8]			
29.	M.Abel ....(GER)	S.Berke 3/6 7/5 9/7		.........................6/3 7/6(5)			
(Q) 30.	S.Berke ....(USA)		L.Zovko [8]				
31.	B.Riby ....(GBR)	L.Zovko [8] 6/2 6/4	.................................6/1 6/3				
32.	L.Zovko [8] ....(CRO)						K.Pless [1]
33.	J.Nieminen [6] ....(FIN)	J.Melzer ....6/7(4) 6/4 6/3					6/2 6/3
34.	J.Melzer ....(AUT)		J.Melzer				
35.	M.Weaver ....(GBR)	A.Bogomolov ....6/4 7/6(3)	.................................6/1 6/4				
(Q) 36.	A.Bogomolov ....(USA)			J.Melzer			
(Q) 37.	Y.Miyazaki ....(JPN)	J.Nelson ....7/6(5) 6/3		.................6/2 4/6 3/0 Ret.			
38.	P.Hammer ....(GER)		M.Fish [10]				
39.	P.Hammer ....(GER)	M.Fish [10] 6/3 6/1	.............................6/4 5/7 6/4				
40.	M.Fish [10] ....(USA)				J.Melzer		
41.	L.Chramosta [12] ....(CZE)	M.A.Hilton 6/4 6/4			............7/6(4) 7/6(0)		
42.	M.A.Hilton ....(GBR)		A.Kracman				
(Q) 43.	A.Kracman ....(SLO)	A.Kracman 7/5 6/3	.................................7/5 6/3				
44.	M.Ormaza ....(ARG)			A.Kracman			
(Q) 45.	J.Froberg ....(SWE)	J.Froberg 6/1 6/2		.........................7/6(4) 7/6(3)			
(Q) 46.	D.Britzen ....(GER)		J.Froberg				
(Q) 47.	L.Pampoulov ....(AUT)	L.Pampoulov ....7/5 7/6(7)	.................................6/4 6/2				
48.	E.Prodon [4] ....(FRA)				A.Mackin		
49.	T.Alves [7] ....(BRA)	A.Mackin ....6/1 7/6(3)			.........................6/3 1/6 6/3		
50.	A.Mackin ....(GBR)		A.Mackin				
51.	F.Hemmes ....(NED)	F.Hemmes 6/2 6/2	.................................6/1 7/6(3)				
52.	A.McDade ....(RSA)			A.Mackin			
53.	A.Banks ....(GBR)	N.Mahut 6/4 6/0		.........................6/3 1/6 6/3			
54.	N.Mahut ....(FRA)		N.Mahut				
55.	H.Furukawa ....(JPN)	H.Furukawa ....6/3 7/6(5)	.............................6/4 4/6 12/10				
(L) 56.	B.Becker ....(GER)				D.Nalbandian [2]		
57.	J-J.Rojer [13] ....(AHO)	L.Harper-Griffith 6/4 6/4			.........................6/4 4/6 7/5		
58.	L.Harper-Griffith ....(USA)		L.Harper-Griffith				
59.	D.Meffert ....(GER)	L.Childs 6/1 6/4	.........................7/6(2) 6/1				
60.	L.Childs ....(GBR)			D.Nalbandian [2]			
61.	M.Ancic ....(CRO)	M.Ancic 4/6 6/4 6/3		.........................4/6 6/4 7/5			
(Q) 62.	U.Kiendl ....(GER)		D.Nalbandian [2]				
63.	T.Enev ....(BUL)	D.Nalbandian [2] 6/4 7/5	.................................6/4 6/4				
64.	D.Nalbandian [2] ....(ARG)						

Semi-Finals: J.Melzer 7/6(7) 6/3; J.Melzer W/O

Final: J.Melzer 7/6(7) 6/3

THE BOYS' DOUBLES CHAMPIONSHIP

Holders: R.Federer and O.Rochus

	First Round	Second Round	Quarter-Finals	Semi-Finals	Final
1.	G.Coria (ARG) & D.Nalbandian (ARG) ....[1]	G.Coria & D.Nalbandian [1] ....7/5 7/6(4)	G.Coria & D.Nalbandian [1]		
2.	J.Gray (GBR) & T.Higgins (GBR)		.........................6/3 6/4	G.Coria & D.Nalbandian [1]	
3.	A.Mackin (GBR) & M.Trudgeon (GBR)	A.Mackin & M.Trudgeon 6/2 6/1		.........................7/6(4) 6/4	
4.	T.Alves (BRA) & T.Nieminen (FIN)				
5.	L.Harper-Griffith (USA) & A.Roddick (USA)	L.Harper-Griffith & A.Roddick ....7/6(2) 6/4	L.Childs & S.Dickson [5]		
6.	C.Gard (ROM) & R.Karanusic (CRO)				
7.	R.Brooks (GBR) & N.Greenhouse (GBR)	L.Childs & S.Dickson [5] 6/4 6/3	.........................6/4 6/4		
8.	L.Childs (GBR) & S.Dickson (GBR) ....[5]				
9.	J.Benneteau (FRA) & N.Mahut (FRA) ....[4]	J.Benneteau & N.Mahut [4] 6/0 4/6 10/8	J.Benneteau & N.Mahut [4]		
10.	M.Ormaza (ARG) & C.Villagran (ARG)		.........................6/1 6/3	M.A.Hilton & J.Nelson	
11.	A.Banks (GBR) & B.Riby (GBR)	A.Banks & B.Riby ....7/6(4) 6/4		.........................7/6(5) 3/6 6/1	
12.	A.Vlaski (YUG) & B.Weir-Smith (RSA)				
13.	M.A.Hilton (GBR) & J.Nelson (GBR)	M.A.Hilton & J.Nelson ....7/6(8) 6/3	M.A.Hilton & J.Nelson		
14.	R.Russell (JAM) & W.Wong (HKG)		.........................6/4 6/4		
15.	T.Davis (USA) & A.Francis (USA)	J.Johansson & L.Zovko [6] ....7/6(4) 6/4			
16.	J.Johansson (SWE) & L.Zovko (CRO) ....[6]				
17.	L.Chramosta (CZE) & J.Hasek (CZE) ....[7]	L.Chramosta & J.Hasek [7] ....6/7(4) 6/4 6/2	T.Enev & J.Nieminen		
18.	F.Hemmes (NED) & L.Pampoulov (AUT)		.........................6/4 6/2	T.Enev & J.Nieminen	
19.	M.Lammer (SUI) & R.Thys (BEL)	T.Enev & J.Nieminen 6/3 6/1		.........................7/6(4) 7/6(4)	
20.	T.Enev (BUL) & J.Nieminen (FIN)				
21.	A.Anderson (RSA) & D.Stegmann (RSA)	A.Anderson & D.Stegmann 6/4 6/4	J.Melzer & K.Pless [3]		
22.	R.Green (GBR) & M.Weaver (GBR)				
23.	S.Berke (USA) & D.Britzen (GER)	J.Melzer & K.Pless [3] 6/3 6/4	.........................6/4 6/4		
24.	J.Melzer (AUT) & K.Pless (DEN) ....[3]				
25.	D.Martin (USA) & J-J.Rojer (AHO) ....[8]	D.Martin & J-J.Rojer [8] ....7/6(4) 6/2	D.Martin & J-J.Rojer [8]		
26.	K.Beck (SVK) & S.Nugent (IRL)			J.De Armas & D.Langre [2]	
27.	M.Ancic (CRO) & A.Kracman (SLO)	H.Furukawa & Y.Miyazaki 4/6 6/3 6/4	.........................4/6 6/1 9/7		
28.	H.Furukawa (JPN) & Y.Miyazaki (JPN)			.........................6/1 7/5	
29.	J-C.Faurel (FRA) & E.Prodon (FRA)	A.Bogomolov & J-P.Fruttero 3/6 6/1 6/1	J.De Armas & D.Langre [2]		
30.	A.Bogomolov (USA) & J-P.Fruttero (USA)				
31.	P.Harboe (CHI) & A.McDade (RSA)	J.De Armas & D.Langre [2] ....7/6(3) 7/6(2)	.........................7/6(3) 7/6(2)		
32.	J.De Armas (VEN) & D.Langre (MEX) ....[2]				

Final: G.Coria & D.Nalbandian [1] 3/6 7/5 17/15; G.Coria & D.Nalbandian [1] 7/5 6/4

Heavy type denotes seeded players. The figure in brackets against names denotes the order in which they have been seeded.
(W) = Wild card. (Q) = Qualifier. (L) = Lucky loser.

The matches are the best of three sets

For both the Girls' Singles *and* the Girls' Doubles Championships, the winners become the holders, for the year only, of a Cup presented by The All England Lawn Tennis and Croquet Club. The winners each receive a miniature Cup and the runners-up receive mementoes.

Holder: Miss K.Srebotnik

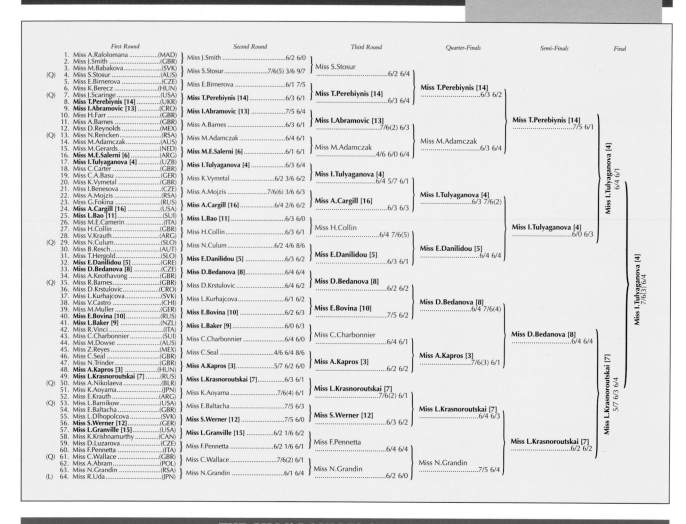

First Round	Second Round	Third Round	Quarter-Finals	Semi-Finals	Final
1. Miss A.Rafolomana ......(MAD)	Miss J.Smith 6/2 6/0	Miss S.Stosur 6/2 6/4	Miss T.Perebiynis [14] 6/3 6/2	Miss T.Perebiynis [14] 7/5 6/1	Miss I.Tulyaganova [4] 6/4 6/1
2. Miss J.Smith ......(GBR)					
3. Miss M.Babakova ......(SVK)	Miss S.Stosur ......7/6(5) 3/6 9/7				
(Q) 4. Miss S.Stosur ......(AUS)					
5. Miss E.Birnerova ......(CZE)	Miss E.Birnerova 6/1 7/5	Miss T.Perebiynis [14] 6/3 6/4			
6. Miss K.Berecz ......(HUN)					
(Q) 7. Miss J.Scaringe ......(USA)	Miss T.Perebiynis [14] 6/3 6/1				
8. Miss T.Perebiynis [14] ......(UKR)					
9. Miss I.Abramovic [13] ......(CRO)	Miss I.Abramovic [13] 7/5 6/4	Miss I.Abramovic [13] 7/6(2) 6/3	Miss M.Adamczak 6/3 6/4		
10. Miss H.Farr ......(GBR)					
11. Miss A.Barnes ......(GBR)	Miss A.Barnes 6/3 6/1				
12. Miss D.Reynolds ......(MEX)					
13. Miss N.Rencken ......(RSA)	Miss M.Adamczak 6/4 6/1	Miss M.Adamczak 4/6 6/0 6/4			
(Q) 14. Miss M.Adamczak ......(AUS)					
15. Miss M.Gerards ......(NED)	Miss M.E.Salerni [6] 6/1 6/1				
16. Miss M.E.Salerni [6] ......(ARG)					
17. Miss I.Tulyaganova [4] ......(UZB)	Miss I.Tulyaganova [4] 6/3 6/4	Miss I.Tulyaganova [4] 6/4 5/7 6/1	Miss I.Tulyaganova [4] 6/3 7/6(2)	Miss I.Tulyaganova [4] 6/0 6/3	
18. Miss C.Carter ......(GBR)					
19. Miss C.A.Basu ......(GER)	Miss K.Vymetal 6/2 3/6 6/2				
20. Miss K.Vymetal ......(GBR)					
21. Miss I.Benesova ......(CZE)	Miss A.Mojzis ......7/6(6) 3/6 6/3	Miss A.Cargill [16] 6/3 6/3			
22. Miss A.Mojzis ......(RSA)					
23. Miss G.Fokina ......(RUS)	Miss A.Cargill [16] 6/4 2/6 6/2				
24. Miss A.Cargill [16] ......(USA)					
25. Miss L.Bao [11] ......(SUI)	Miss L.Bao [11] 6/3 6/0	Miss H.Collin 6/4 7/6(5)	Miss E.Danilidou [5] 6/4 6/4		
26. Miss M.E.Camerin ......(ITA)					
27. Miss H.Collin ......(GBR)	Miss H.Collin 6/3 6/1				
28. Miss V.Krauth ......(ARG)					
(Q) 29. Miss N.Culum ......(SLO)	Miss N.Culum 6/2 4/6 8/6	Miss E.Danilidou [5] 6/3 6/1			
30. Miss B.Resch ......(AUT)					
31. Miss T.Hergold ......(SLO)	Miss E.Danilidou [5] 6/3 6/2				
32. Miss E.Danilidou [5] ......(GRE)					
33. Miss D.Bedanova [8] ......(CZE)	Miss D.Bedanova [8] 6/4 6/4	Miss D.Bedanova [8] 6/2 6/2	Miss D.Bedanova [8] 6/4 7/6(4)	Miss D.Bedanova [8] 6/4 6/4	
34. Miss A.Keothavong ......(GBR)					
(Q) 35. Miss R.Barnes ......(GBR)	Miss D.Krstulovic 6/4 6/2				
36. Miss D.Krstulovic ......(CRO)					
37. Miss L.Kurhajcova ......(SVK)	Miss L.Kurhajcova 6/1 6/2	Miss E.Bovina [10] 7/5 6/2			
38. Miss V.Castro ......(CHI)					
39. Miss M.Muller ......(GER)	Miss E.Bovina [10] 6/2 6/3				
40. Miss E.Bovina [10] ......(RUS)					
41. Miss L.Baker [9] ......(NZL)	Miss L.Baker [9] 6/0 6/3	Miss C.Charbonnier 6/4 6/0	Miss A.Kapros [3] 7/6(3) 6/1		
42. Miss R.Vinci ......(ITA)					
43. Miss C.Charbonnier ......(SUI)	Miss C.Charbonnier 6/4 6/0				
44. Miss M.Dowse ......(AUS)					
45. Miss Z.Reyes ......(MEX)	Miss C.Seal 4/6 6/4 8/6	Miss A.Kapros [3] 6/2 6/2			
46. Miss C.Seal ......(GBR)					
47. Miss N.Trinder ......(GBR)	Miss A.Kapros [3] 5/7 6/2 6/0				
48. Miss A.Kapros [3] ......(HUN)					
49. Miss L.Krasnoroutskai [7] ......(RUS)	Miss L.Krasnoroutskai [7] 6/3 6/1	Miss L.Krasnoroutskai [7] 7/6(2) 6/1	Miss L.Krasnoroutskai [7] 6/4 6/3	Miss L.Krasnoroutskai [7] 6/2 6/2	Miss L.Krasnoroutskai [7] 5/7 6/3 6/4
(Q) 50. Miss A.Nikolaeva ......(BLR)					
51. Miss K.Aoyama ......(JPN)	Miss K.Aoyama ......7/6(4) 6/1				
52. Miss E.Krauth ......(ARG)					
(Q) 53. Miss L.Barnikow ......(USA)	Miss E.Baltacha 7/5 6/3	Miss S.Werner [12] 6/3 6/2			
54. Miss E.Baltacha ......(GBR)					
55. Miss L.Dlhopolcova ......(SVK)	Miss S.Werner [12] 7/5 6/0				
56. Miss S.Werner [12] ......(GER)					
57. Miss L.Granville [15] ......(USA)	Miss L.Granville [15] 6/2 1/6 6/2	Miss F.Pennetta 6/4 6/4	Miss N.Grandin 7/5 6/4		
58. Miss K.Krishnamurthy ......(CAN)					
59. Miss D.Luzarova ......(CZE)	Miss F.Pennetta 6/2 1/6 6/1				
60. Miss F.Pennetta ......(ITA)					
(Q) 61. Miss C.Wallace ......(GBR)	Miss C.Wallace ......7/6(2) 6/1	Miss N.Grandin 6/2 6/0			
62. Miss A.Abram ......(POL)					
63. Miss N.Grandin ......(RSA)	Miss N.Grandin 6/1 6/4				
(L) 64. Miss R.Uda ......(JPN)					

Holders: Miss E.Dryberg and Miss J.Kostanic

First Round	Second Round	Quarter-Finals	Semi-Finals	Final
1. Miss F.Pennetta (ITA) & Miss R.Vinci (ITA) ......[1]	Miss F.Pennetta & Miss R.Vinci [1]	Miss F.Pennetta & Miss R.Vinci [1] 2/6 6/2 6/2	Miss F.Pennetta & Miss R.Vinci [1] 7/5 6/4	Miss T.Perebiynis & Miss I.Tulyaganova [7] 6/3 6/4
2. bye				
3. Miss M.Adamczak (AUS) & Miss M.Dowse (AUS)	Miss M.Adamczak & Miss M.Dowse 6/3 6/1			
4. Miss E.Baltacha (GBR) & Miss C.Seal (GBR)				
5. Miss R.Barnes (GBR) & A.Keothavong (GBR)	Miss G.Fokina & Miss L.Krasnoroutskai 6/0 6/2	Miss G.Fokina & Miss L.Krasnoroutskai 6/4 6/3		
6. Miss G.Fokina (RUS) & Miss L.Krasnoroutskai (RUS)				
7. Miss A.Hawkins (GBR) & Miss E.Webley-Smith (GBR)	Miss N.Culum & Miss S.Stone [8] 6/4 6/1			
8. Miss N.Culum (SLO) & Miss S.Stone (AUS) ......[8]				
9. Miss E.Krauth (ARG) & Miss V.Krauth (ARG) ......[3]	Miss E.Krauth & Miss V.Krauth [3] 4/6 6/3 6/2	Miss L.Baker & Miss K.Berecz 7/6(3) 6/0	Miss T.Perebiynis & Miss I.Tulyaganova [7] 6/3 6/4	
10. Miss I.Benesova (CZE) & Miss E.Birnerova (CZE)				
11. Miss L.Baker (NZL) & Miss K.Berecz (HUN)	Miss L.Baker & Miss K.Berecz 6/0 6/2			
12. Miss H.Farr (GBR) & Miss S.Gregg (GBR)				
13. Miss K.Krishnamurthy (CAN) & Miss D.Reynolds (MEX)	Miss L.Bao & Miss C.Charbonnier 6/1 6/3	Miss T.Perebiynis & Miss I.Tulyaganova [7] 6/1 4/6 6/2		
14. Miss L.Bao (SUI) & Miss C.Charbonnier (SUI)				
15. Miss J.Smith (GBR) & Miss K.Vymetal (GBR)	Miss T.Perebiynis & Miss I.Tulyaganova [7] 4/6 6/1 8/6			
16. Miss T.Perebiynis (UKR) & Miss I.Tulyaganova (UZB) [7]				
17. Miss A.Cargill (USA) & Miss L.Granville (USA) ......[6]	Miss A.Cargill & Miss L.Granville [6] 7/5 6/4	Miss A.Cargill & Miss L.Granville [6] 7/6(5) 6/4	Miss A.Cargill & Miss L.Granville [6] 6/2 6/1	Miss D.Bedanova & Miss M.E.Salerni [2] 6/1 2/6 6/2
18. Miss L.Dlhopolcova (SVK) & Miss L.Kurhajcova (SVK)				
19. Miss M.Babakova (SVK) & Miss V.Castro (CHI)	Miss M.Babakova & Miss V.Castro 6/3 6/4			
20. Miss L.Barnikow (USA) & Miss J.Scaringe (USA)				
21. Miss E.Bovina (RUS) & Miss M.Gerards (NED)	Miss E.Bovina & Miss M.Gerards 6/2 6/4	Miss E.Bovina & Miss M.Gerards 6/2 6/3		
22. Miss C.Wallace (GBR) & Miss L.Wood (GBR)				
23. Miss A.Abram (POL) & Miss B.Resch (AUT)	Miss A.Kapros & Miss A.Mojzis [4] ......w/o			
24. Miss A.Kapros (HUN) & Miss A.Mojzis (RSA) ......[4]				
25. Miss N.Grandin (RSA) & Miss N.Rencken (RSA) ......[5]	Miss N.Grandin & Miss N.Rencken [5] 6/4 6/2	Miss N.Grandin & Miss N.Rencken [5] 6/2 6/1	Miss D.Bedanova & Miss M.E.Salerni [2] 7/5 6/4	
26. Miss D.Luzarova (CZE) & Miss S.Stosur (AUS)				
27. Miss A.Rafolomana (MAD) & Miss Z.Reyes (MEX)	Miss A.Barnes & Miss N.Trinder ......6/7(1) 6/4 6/3			
28. Miss A.Barnes (GBR) & Miss N.Trinder (GBR)				
29. Miss K.Aoyama (JPN) & Miss R.Uda (JPN)	Miss K.Aoyama & Miss R.Uda 6/3 3/6 6/3	Miss D.Bedanova & Miss M.E.Salerni [2] 6/3 6/1		
30. Miss I.Abramovic (CRO) & Miss D.Krstulovic (CRO)				
31. Miss H.Collin (GBR) & Miss T.Hergold (SLO)	Miss D.Bedanova & Miss M.E.Salerni [2] ......7/6(8) 6/7(1) 6/3			
32. Miss D.Bedanova (CZE) & Miss M.E.Salerni (ARG) ......[2]				

Heavy type denotes seeded players. The figure in brackets against names denotes the order in which they have been seeded.
(W) = Wild card. (Q) = Qualifier. (L) = Lucky loser.

The matches are the best of three sets

Champions and Runners-up

Year	Champion / Runner-up	Year	Champion / Runner-up	Year	Champion / Runner-up	Year	Champion / Runner-up	Year	Champion / Runner-up
1877	S. W. Gore / W. C. Marshall	1909	A. W. Gore / M. J. G. Ritchie	1929	H. Cochet / J. Borotra	1951	R. Savitt / K. McGregor	1967	J. D. Newcombe / W. P. Bungert
1878	P. F. Hadow / S. W. Gore	1910	A. F. Wilding / A. W. Gore	1930	W. T. Tilden / W. Allison	1952	F. A. Sedgman / J. Drobny	1968	R. Laver / A. D. Roche
★ 1879	J. T. Hartley / V. St. L. Goold	1911	A. F. Wilding / H. Roper Barrett	★ 1931	S. B. Wood / F. X. Shields	★ 1953	V. Seixas / K. Nielsen	1969	R. Laver / J. D. Newcombe
1880	J. T. Hartley / H. F. Lawford	1912	A. F. Wilding / A. W. Gore	1932	H. E. Vines / H. W. Austin	1954	J. Drobny / K. R. Rosewall	1970	J. D. Newcombe / K. R. Rosewall
1881	W. Renshaw / J. T. Hartley	1913	A. F. Wilding / M. E. McLoughlin	1933	J. H. Crawford / H. E. Vines	1955	T. Trabert / K. Nielsen	1971	J. D. Newcombe / S. R. Smith
1882	W. Renshaw / E. Renshaw	1914	N. E. Brookes / A. F. Wilding	1934	F. J. Perry / J. H. Crawford	★ 1956	L. A. Hoad / K. R. Rosewall	★ 1972	S. R. Smith / I. Nastase
1883	W. Renshaw / E. Renshaw							★ 1973	J. Kodes / A. Metreveli
1884	W. Renshaw / H. F. Lawford							1974	J. S. Connors / K. R. Rosewall
1885	W. Renshaw / H. F. Lawford							1975	A. R. Ashe / J. S. Connors
1886	W. Renshaw / H. F. Lawford							1976	B. Borg / I. Nastase
★ 1887	H. F. Lawford / E. Renshaw							1977	B. Borg / J. S. Connors
1888	E. Renshaw / H. F. Lawford							1978	B. Borg / J. S. Connors
1889	W. Renshaw / E. Renshaw							1979	B. Borg / R. Tanner
1890	W. J. Hamilton / W. Renshaw							1980	B. Borg / J. P. McEnroe
★ 1891	W. Baddeley / J. Pim							1981	J. P. McEnroe / B. Borg
1892	W. Baddeley / J. Pim							1982	J. S. Connors / J. P. McEnroe
1893	J. Pim / W. Baddeley							1983	J. P. McEnroe / C. J. Lewis
1894	J. Pim / W. Baddeley							1984	J. P. McEnroe / J. S. Connors
★ 1895	W. Baddeley / W. V. Eaves							1985	B. Becker / K. Curren
1896	H. S. Mahony / W. Baddeley							1986	B. Becker / I. Lendl
1897	R. F. Doherty / H. S. Mahony							1987	P. Cash / I. Lendl
1898	R. F. Doherty / H. L . Doherty							1988	S. Edberg / B. Becker
1899	R. F. Doherty / A. W. Gore	1919	G. L. Patterson / N. E. Brookes	1935	F. J. Perry / G. von Cramm	1957	L. A. Hoad / A. J. Cooper	1989	B. Becker / S. Edberg
1900	R. F. Doherty / S. H. Smith	1920	W. T. Tilden / G. L. Patterson	1936	F. J. Perry / G. von Cramm	★ 1958	A. J. Cooper / N. A. Fraser	1990	S. Edberg / B. Becker
1901	A. W. Gore / R. F. Doherty	1921	W. T. Tilden / B. I. C. Norton	★ 1937	J. D. Budge / G. von Cramm	★ 1959	A. Olmedo / R. Laver	1991	M. Stich / B. Becker
1902	H. L. Doherty / A. W. Gore	★† 1922	G. L. Patterson / R. Lycett	1938	J. D. Budge / H. W. Austin	★ 1960	N. A. Fraser / R. Laver	1992	A. Agassi / G. Ivanisevic
1903	H. L. Doherty / F. L. Riseley	★ 1923	W. M. Johnston / F. T. Hunter	★ 1939	R. L. Riggs / E. T. Cooke	1961	R. Laver / C. R. McKinley	1993	P. Sampras / J. Courier
1904	H. L. Doherty / F. L. Riseley	★ 1924	J. Borotra / R. Lacoste	★ 1946	Y. Petra / G. E. Brown	1962	R. Laver / M. F. Mulligan	1994	P. Sampras / G. Ivanisevic
1905 –	H. L. Doherty / N. E. Brookes	1925	R. Lacoste / J. Borotra	1947	J. Kramer / T. Brown	★ 1963	C. R. McKinley / F. S. Stolle	1995	P. Sampras / B. Becker
1906 –	H. L. Doherty / F. L. Riseley	1926	J. Borotra / H. Kinsey	★ 1948	R. Falkenburg / J. E. Bromwich	1964	R. Emerson / F. S. Stolle	1996	R. Krajicek / M. Washington
★ 1907 –	N. E. Brookes / A. W. Gore	1927	H. Cochet / J. Borotra	1949	F. R. Schroeder / J. Drobny	1965	R. Emerson / F. S. Stolle	1997	P. Sampras / C. Pioline
★ 1908 –	A. W. Gore / H. Roper Barrett	1928	R. Lacoste / H. Cochet	★ 1950	B. Patty / F. A. Sedgman	1966	M. Santana / R. D. Ralston	1998	P. Sampras / G. Ivanisevic

NOTE: For the years 1913, 1914 and 1919-23 inclusive the Championship Roll includes the 'World's Championship on Grass' granted to The Lawn Tennis Association by The International Lawn Tennis Federation. This title was then abolished and commencing in 1924 they became The Official Lawn Tennis Championships recognised by The International Lawn Tennis Federation. Prior to 1922 the holders in the singles events and the gentlemen's doubles did not compete in The Championships but met the winners of these events in the Challenge Rounds. † Challenge Round abolished; holders subsequently played through. *The holder did not defend the title.

Champions and Runners-up

1884	Miss M. Watson / Miss L. Watson	1914	Mrs. Lambert Chambers / Mrs. D. R. Larcombe	1933	Mrs. F. S. Moody / Miss D. E. Round	1954	Miss M. Connolly / Miss L. Brough	1969	Mrs. P. F. Jones / Mrs. L. W. King

1884   Miss M. Watson / Miss L. Watson
1885   Miss M. Watson / Miss B. Bingley
1886   Miss B. Bingley / Miss M. Watson
1887   Miss L. Dod / Miss B. Bingley
1888   Miss L. Dod / Mrs. G. W. Hillyard
★1889 Mrs. G. W. Hillyard / Miss L. Rice
★1890 Miss L. Rice / Miss M. Jacks
★1891 Miss L. Dod / Mrs. G. W. Hillyard
1892   Miss L. Dod / Mrs. G. W. Hillyard
1893   Miss L. Dod / Mrs. G. W. Hillyard
★1894 Mrs. G. W. Hillyard / Miss E. L. Austin
★1895 Miss C. Cooper / Miss H. Jackson
1896   Miss C. Cooper / Mrs. W. H. Pickering
1897   Mrs. G. W. Hillyard / Miss C. Cooper
★1898 Miss C. Cooper / Miss L Martin
1899   Mrs. G. W. Hillyard / Miss C. Cooper
1900   Mrs. G. W. Hillyard / Miss C. Cooper
1901   Mrs. A. Sterry / Mrs. G. W. Hillyard
1902   Miss M. E. Robb / Mrs. A. Sterry
★1903 Miss D. K. Douglass / Miss E. W. Thomson
1904   Miss D. K. Douglass / Mrs. A. Sterry
1905   Miss M. Sutton / Miss D. K. Douglass
1906   Miss D. K. Douglass / Miss M. Sutton
1907   Miss M. Sutton / Mrs. Lambert Chambers
★1908 Mrs. A. Sterry / Miss A. M. Morton
★1909 Miss D. P. Boothby / Miss A. M. Morton
1910   Mrs. Lambert Chambers / Miss D. P. Boothby
1911   Mrs. Lambert Chambers / Miss D. P. Boothby
★1912 Mrs. D. R. Larcombe / Mrs. A. Sterry
★1913 Mrs. Lambert Chambers / Mrs. R. J. McNair

1914   Mrs. Lambert Chambers / Mrs. D. R. Larcombe
1919   Mlle. S. Lenglen / Mrs. Lambert Chambers
1920   Mlle. S. Lenglen / Mrs. Lambert Chambers
1921   Mlle. S. Lenglen / Miss E. Ryan
†1922 Mlle. S. Lenglen / Mrs. F. Mallory
1923   Mlle. S. Lenglen / Miss K. McKane
1924   Miss K. McKane / Miss H. Wills
1925   Mlle. S. Lenglen / Miss J. Fry
1926   Mrs. L. A. Godfree / Sta. L. de Alvarez
1927   Miss H. Wills / Sta. L. de Alvarez
1928   Miss H. Wills / Sta. L. de Alvarez
1929   Miss H. Wills / Miss H. H. Jacobs
1930   Mrs. F. S. Moody / Miss E. Ryan
★1931 Fraulein C. Aussem / Fraulein H. Krahwinkel
★1932 Mrs. F. S. Moody / Miss H. H. Jacobs

1933   Mrs. F. S. Moody / Miss D. E. Round
★1934 Miss D. E. Round / Miss H. H. Jacobs
1935   Mrs. F. S. Moody / Miss H. H. Jacobs
★1936 Miss H. H. Jacobs / Frau. S. Sperling
1937   Miss D. E. Round / Miss J. Jedrzejowska
★1938 Mrs. F. S. Moody / Miss H. H. Jacobs
★1939 Miss A. Marble / Miss K. E. Stammers
★1946 Miss P. Betz / Miss L. Brough
★1947 Miss M. Osborne / Miss D. Hart
1948   Miss L. Brough / Miss D. Hart
1949   Miss L. Brough / Mrs. W. du Pont
1950   Miss L. Brough / Mrs. W. du Pont
1951   Miss D. Hart / Miss S. Fry
1952   Miss M. Connolly / Miss L. Brough
1953   Miss M. Connolly / Miss D. Hart

1954   Miss M. Connolly / Miss L. Brough
★1955 Miss L. Brough / Mrs. J. G. Fleitz
1956   Miss S. Fry / Miss A. Buxton
★1957 Miss A. Gibson / Miss D. R. Hard
1958   Miss A. Gibson / Miss A. Mortimer
★1959 Miss M. E. Bueno / Miss D. R. Hard
1960   Miss M. E. Bueno / Miss S. Reynolds
★1961 Miss A. Mortimer / Miss C. C. Truman
1962   Mrs. J. R. Susman / Mrs. V. Sukova
★1963 Miss M. Smith / Miss B. J. Moffitt
1964   Miss M. E. Bueno / Miss M. Smith
1965   Miss M. Smith / Miss M. E. Bueno
1966   Mrs. L. W. King / Miss M. E. Bueno
1967   Mrs. L. W. King / Mrs. P. F. Jones
1968   Mrs. L. W. King / Miss J. A. M. Tegart

1969   Mrs. P. F. Jones / Mrs. L. W. King
★1970 Mrs. B. M. Court / Mrs. L. W. King
1971   Miss E. F. Goolagong / Mrs. B. M. Court
1972   Mrs. L. W. King / Miss E. F. Goolagong
1973   Mrs. L. W. King / Miss C. M. Evert
1974   Miss C. M. Evert / Mrs. O. Morozova
1975   Mrs. L. W. King / Mrs. R. Cawley
★1976 Miss C. M. Evert / Mrs. R. Cawley
1977   Miss S. V. Wade / Miss B. F. Stove
1978   Miss M. Navratilova / Miss C. M. Evert
1979   Miss M. Navratilova / Mrs. J. M. Lloyd
1980   Mrs. R. Cawley / Mrs. J. M. Lloyd
1981   Mrs. J. M. Lloyd / Miss H. Mandlikova
1982   Miss M. Navratilova / Mrs. J. M. Lloyd
1983   Miss M. Navratilova / Miss A. Jaeger
1984   Miss M. Navratilova / Mrs. J. M. Lloyd
1985   Miss M. Navratilova / Mrs. J. M. Lloyd
1986   Miss M. Navratilova / Miss H. Mandlikova
1987   Miss M. Navratilova / Miss S. Graf
1988   Miss S. Graf / Miss M. Navratilova
1989   Miss S. Graf / Miss M. Navratilova
1990   Miss M. Navratilova / Miss Z. Garrison
1991   Miss S. Graf / Miss G. Sabatini
1992   Miss S. Graf / Miss M. Seles
1993   Miss S. Graf / Miss J. Novotna
1994   Miss C. Martinez / Miss M. Navratilova
1995   Miss S. Graf / Miss A. Sanchez Vicario
1996   Miss S. Graf / Miss A. Sanchez Vicario
1997   Miss M. Hingis / Miss J. Novotna
1998   Miss J. Novotna / Miss N. Tauziat

MAIDEN NAMES OF LADY CHAMPIONS

In the tables the following have been recorded in both married and single identities.

Mrs. R. Cawley .... Miss E. F. Goolagong
Mrs. Lambert Chambers .... Miss D. K. Douglass
Mrs. B. M. Court .... Miss M. Smith
Mrs. B. C. Covell .... Miss P. L. Howkins
Mrs. D. E. Dalton .... Miss J. A. M. Tegart
Mrs. W. du Pont .... Miss M. Osborne
Mrs. L. A. Godfree .... Miss K. McKane
Mrs. H. F. Gourlay Cawley .... Miss H. F. Gourlay

Mrs. G. W. Hillyard .... Miss B. Bingley
Mrs. P. F. Jones .... Miss A. S. Haydon
Mrs. L. W. King .... Miss B. J. Moffitt
Mrs. M. R. King .... Miss P. E. Mudford
Mrs. D. R. Larcombe .... Miss E. W. Thomson
Mrs. J. M. Lloyd .... Miss C. M. Evert

Mrs. F. S. Moody .... Miss H. Wills
Mrs. O. Morozova .... Miss O. Morozova
Mrs. L. E. G. Price .... Miss S. Reynolds
Mrs. G. E. Reid .... Miss K. Melville
Mrs. P. D. Smylie .... Miss E. M. Sayers
Frau. S. Sperling .... Fraulein H. Krahwinkel
Mrs. A. Sterry .... Miss C. Cooper
Mrs. J. R. Susman .... Miss K. Hantze

GENTLEMEN'S DOUBLES

1879 L. R. Erskine and H. F. Lawford
F. Durant and G. E . Tabor
1880 W. Renshaw and E. Renshaw
O. E. Woodhouse and C. J. Cole
1881 W. Renshaw and E. Renshaw
W. J. Down and H. Vaughan
1882 J. T. Hartley and R. T. Richardson
J. G. Horn and C. B. Russell
1883 C. W. Grinstead and C. E. Welldon
C. B. Russell and R. T. Milford
1884 W. Renshaw and E. Renshaw
E. W. Lewis and E. L Williams
1885 W. Renshaw and E. Renshaw
C. E. Farrer and A. J. Stanley
1886 W. Renshaw and E. Renshaw
C. E. Farrer and A. J. Stanley
1887 P. Bowes-Lyon and H. W. W. Wilberforce
J. H. Crispe and E. Barratt Smith
1888 W. Renshaw and E. Renshaw
P. Bowes-Lyon and H. W. W. Wilberforce
1889 W. Renshaw and E. Renshaw
E. W. Lewis and G. W. Hillyard
1890 J. Pim and F. O. Stoker
E. W. Lewis and G. W. Hillyard
1891 W. Baddeley and H. Baddeley
J. Pim and F. O. Stoker
1892 H. S. Barlow and E. W. Lewis
W. Baddeley and H. Baddeley
1893 J. Pim and F. O. Stoker
E. W. Lewis and H. S. Barlow
1894 W. Baddeley and H. Baddeley
H. S. Barlow and C. H. Martin
1895 W. Baddeley and H. Baddeley
E. W. Lewis and W. V. Eaves
1896 W. Baddeley and H. Baddeley
R. F. Doherty and H. A. Nisbet
1897 R. F. Doherty and H. L. Doherty
W. Baddeley and H. Baddeley
1898 R. F. Doherty and H. L . Doherty
H. A. Nisbet and C. Hobart
1899 R. F. Doherty and H. L. Doherty
H. A. Nisbet and C. Hobart
1900 R. F. Doherty and H. L. Doherty
H. Roper Barrett and H. A. Nisbet
1901 R. F. Doherty and H. L. Doherty
Dwight Davis and Holcombe Ward
1902 S. H. Smith and F. L. Riseley
R. F. Doherty and H. L. Doherty
1903 R. F. Doherty and H. L. Doherty
S. H. Smith and F. L. Riseley
1904 R. F. Doherty and H. L. Doherty
S. H. Smith and F. L. Riseley
1905 R. F. Doherty and H. L. Doherty
S. H. Smith and F. L. Riseley
1906 S. H. Smith and F. L. Riseley
R. F. Doherty and H. L. Doherty
1907 N. E. Brooks and A. F. Wilding
B. C. Wright and K. H. Behr
1908 A. F. Wilding and M. J. G. Ritchie
A. W. Gore and H. Roper Barrett
1909 A. W. Gore and H. Roper Barrett
S. N. Doust and H. A. Parker
1910 A. F. Wilding and M. J. G. Ritchie
A. W. Gore and H. Roper Barrett
1911 M. Decugis and A. H. Gobert
M. J. G. Ritchie and A. F. Wilding
1912 H. Roper Barrett and C. P. Dixon
M. Decugis and A. H. Gobert
1913 H. Roper Barrett and C. P. Dixon
F. W. Rahe and H. Kleinschroth
1914 N. E. Brookes and A. F. Wilding
H. Roper Barrett and C. P. Dixon
1919 R. V. Thomas and P. O'Hara-Wood
R. Lycett and R. W. Heath
1920 R. N. Williams and C. S. Garland
A. R. F. Kingscote and J. C. Parke
1921 R. Lycett and M. Woosnam
F. G. Lowe and A. H. Lowe
1922 R. Lycett and J. O. Anderson
G. L. Patterson and P. O'Hara-Wood
1923 R. Lycett and L. A. Godfree
Count de Gomar and E. Flaquer
1924 F. T. Hunter and V. Richards
R. N. Williams and W. M. Washburn
1925 J. Borotra and R. Lacoste
J. Hennessey and R. Casey
1926 H. Cochet and J. Brugnon
V. Richards and H. Kinsey
1927 F. T. Hunter and W. T. Tilden
J. Brugnon and H. Cochet
1928 H. Cochet and J. Brugnon
G. L. Patterson and J. B. Hawkes
1929 W. Allison and J. Van Ryn
J. C. Gregory and I. G. Collins
1930 W. Allison and J. Van Ryn
J. H. Doeg and G. M. Lott
1931 G. M Lott and J. Van Ryn
H. Cochet and J. Brugnon
1932 J. Borotra and J. Brugnon
G. P. Hughes and F. J. Perry
1933 J. Borotra and J. Brugnon
R. Nunoi and J. Satoh
1934 G. M. Lott and L. R. Stoefen
J. Borotra and J. Brugnon
1935 J. H. Crawford and A. K . Quist
W. Allison and J. Van Ryn
1936 G. P. Hughes and C. R. D. Tuckey
C. E. Hare and F. H. D. Wilde
1937 J. D. Budge and G. Mako
G. P. Hughes and C. R. D. Tuckey
1938 J. D. Budge and G. Mako
H. Henkel and G. von Metaxa
1939 R. L. Riggs and E. T. Cooke
C. E. Hare and F. H. D. Wilde
1946 T. Brown and J. Kramer
G. E. Brown and D. Pails
1947 R. Falkenburg and J. Kramer
A. J. Mottram and O. W. Sidwell
1948 J. E. Bromwich and F. A. Sedgman
T. Brown and G. Mulloy
1949 R. Gonzales and F. Parker
G. Mulloy and F. R. Schroeder
1950 J. E. Bromwich and A. K. Quist
G. E. Brown and O. W. Sidwell
1951 K. McGregor and F. A. Sedgman
J. Drobny and E. W. Sturgess
1952 K. McGregor and F. A. Sedgman
V. Seixas and E. W. Sturgess
1953 L. A. Hoad and K. R. Rosewall
R. N. Hartwig and M. G. Rose
1954 R. N. Hartwig and M. G. Rose
V. Seixas and T. Trabert
1955 R. N. Hartwig and L. A. Hoad
N. A. Fraser and K. R. Rosewall
1956 L. A. Hoad and K. R. Rosewall
N. Pietrangeli and O. Sirola
1957 G. Mulloy and B. Patty
N. A. Fraser and L. A. Hoad
1958 S. Davidson and U. Schmidt
A. J. Cooper and N. A. Fraser
1959 R. Emerson and N. A. Fraser
R. Laver and R. Mark
1960 R. H. Osuna and R. D. Ralston
M. G. Davies and R. K. Wilson
1961 R. Emerson and N. A. Fraser
R. A. J. Hewitt and F. S. Stolle
1962 R. A. J. Hewitt and F. S. Stolle
B. Jovanovic and N. Pilic
1963 R. H. Osuna and A. Palafox
J. C. Barclay and P. Darmon
1964 R. A. J. Hewitt and F. S. Stolle
R. Emerson and K. N. Fletcher
1965 J. D. Newcombe and A. D. Roche
K. N. Fletcher and R. A. J. Hewitt
1966 K. N. Fletcher and J. D. Newcombe
W. W. Bowrey and O. K. Davidson
1967 R. A. J. Hewitt and F. D. McMillan
R. Emerson and K. N. Fletcher
1968 J. D. Newcombe and A. D. Roche
K. R. Rosewall and F. S. Stolle
1969 J. D. Newcombe and A. D. Roche
T. S. Okker and M. C. Reissen
1970 J. D. Newcombe and A. D. Roche
K. R. Rosewall and F. S. Stolle
1971 R. S. Emerson and R. G. Laver
A. R. Ashe and R. D. Ralston
1972 R. A. J. Hewitt and F. D. McMillan
S. R. Smith and E. J. van Dillen
1973 J. S. Connors and I. Nastase
J. R. Cooper and N. A. Fraser
1974 J. D. Newcombe and A. D. Roche
R. C. Lutz and S. R. Smith
1975 V. Gerulaitis and A. Mayer
C. Dowdeswell and A. J. Stone
1976 B. E. Gottfried and R. Ramirez
R. L. Case and G. Masters
1977 R. L. Case and G. Masters
J. G. Alexander and P. C. Dent
1978 R. A. J. Hewitt and F. D. McMillan
P. Fleming and J. P. McEnroe
1979 P. Fleming and J. P . McEnroe
B. E. Gottfried and R. Ramirez
1980 P. McNamara and P. McNamee
R. C. Lutz and S. R. Smith
1981 P. Fleming and J. P. McEnroe
R. C. Lutz and S. R. Smith
1982 P. McNamara and P. McNamee
P. Fleming and J. P. McEnroe
1983 P. Fleming and J. P McEnroe
T. E. Gullikson and T. R. Gullikson
1984 P. Fleming and J. P. McEnroe
P. Cash and P. McNamee
1985 H. P. Guenthardt and B. Taroczy
P. Cash and J. B. Fitzgerald
1986 J. Nystrom and M. Wilander
G. Donnelly and P. Fleming
1987 K. Flach and R. Seguso
S. Casal and E. Sanchez
1988 K. Flach and R. Seguso
J. B. Fitzgerald and A. Jarryd
1989 J. B. Fitzgerald and A. Jarryd
R. Leach and J. Pugh
1990 R. Leach and J. Pugh
P. Aldrich and D. T. Visser
1991 J. B. Fitzgerald and A. Jarryd
J. Frana and L. Lavalle
1992 J. P. McEnroe and M. Stich
J. Grabb and R. A. Reneberg
1993 T. A. Woodbridge and M. Woodforde
G. Connell and P. Galbraith
1994 T. A. Woodbridge and M. Woodforde
G. Connell and P. Galbraith
1995 T. A. Woodbridge and M. Woodforde
R. Leach and S. Melville
1996 T. A. Woodbridge and M. Woodforde
B. Black and G. Connell
1997 T. A. Woodbridge and M. Woodforde
J. Eltingh and P. Haarhuis
1998 J. Eltingh and P. Haarhuis
T. A. Woodbridge and M. Woodforde

LADIES' DOUBLES

1913 Mrs. R. J. McNair and Miss D. P. Boothby
Mrs. A. Sterry and Mrs. Lambert Chambers
1914 Miss E. Ryan and Miss A. M. Morton
Mrs. D. R. Larcombe and Mrs. F. J. Hannam
1919 Mlle. S. Lenglen and Miss E. Ryan
Mrs. Lambert Chambers and Mrs. D. R. Larcombe
1920 Mlle. S. Lenglen and Miss E. Ryan
Mrs. Lambert Chambers and Mrs. D. R. Larcombe
1921 Mlle. S. Lenglen and Miss E. Ryan
Mrs. A. E. Beamish and Mrs. G. E. Peacock
1922 Mlle. S. Lenglen and Miss E. Ryan
Mrs. A. D. Stocks and Miss K. McKane
1923 Mlle. S. Lenglen and Miss E. Ryan
Miss J. Austin and Miss E. L. Colyer
1924 Mrs. H. Wightman and Miss H. Wills
Mrs. B. C. Covell and Miss K. McKane
1925 Mlle. S. Lenglen and Miss E. Ryan
Mrs. A. V. Bridge and Mrs. C. G. McIlquham
1926 Miss E. Ryan and Miss M. K. Browne
Mrs. L. A. Godfree and Miss E. L. Colyer
1927 Miss H. Wills and Miss E. Ryan
Miss E. L. Heine and Mrs. G. E. Peacock
1928 Mrs. Holcroft-Watson and Miss P. Saunders
Miss E. H. Harvey and Miss E. Bennett
1929 Mrs. Holcroft-Watson and Mrs. L. R. C. Michell
Mrs. B. C. Covell and Mrs. D. C. Shepherd-Barron
1930 Mrs. F. S. Moody and Miss E. Ryan
Miss E. Cross and Miss S. Palfrey
1931 Mrs. D. C. Shepherd-Barron and Miss P. E. Mudford
Mlle. D. Metaxa and Mlle. J. Sigart
1932 Mlle. D. Metaxa and Mlle. J. Sigart
Miss E. Ryan and Miss H. H. Jacobs
1933 Mme. R. Mathieu and Miss E. Ryan
Miss F. James and Miss A. M. Yorke
1934 Mme. R. Mathieu and Miss E. Ryan
Mrs. D. Andrus and Mme. S. Henrotin
1935 Miss F. James and Miss K. E. Stammers
Mme. R. Mathieu and Frau. S. Sperling
1936 Miss F. James and Miss K. E. Stammers
Mrs. S. P. Fabyan and Miss H. H. Jacobs
1937 Mme. R. Mathieu and Miss A. M. Yorke
Mrs. M. R. King and Mrs. J. B. Pittman
1938 Mrs. S. P. Fabyan and Miss A. Marble
Mme. R. Mathieu and Miss A. M. Yorke
1939 Mrs S. P. Fabyan and Miss A. Marble
Miss H. H. Jacobs and Miss A. M. Yorke
1946 Miss L. Brough and Miss M. Osborne
Miss P. Betz and Miss D. Hart
1947 Miss D. Hart and Mrs. P. C. Todd
Miss L. Brough and Miss M. Osborne
1948 Miss L. Brough and Mrs. W. du Pont
Miss D. Hart and Mrs. P. C. Todd
1949 Miss L. Brough and Mrs. W. du Pont
Miss G. Moran and Mrs. P. C. Todd
1950 Miss L. Brough and Mrs. W. du Pont
Miss S. Fry and Miss D. Hart
1951 Miss S. Fry and Miss D. Hart
Miss L. Brough and Mrs. W. du Pont
1952 Miss S. Fry and Miss D. Hart
Miss L. Brough and Miss M. Connolly
1953 Miss S. Fry and Miss D. Hart
Miss M. Connolly and Miss J. Sampson
1954 Miss L. Brough and Mrs. W. du Pont
Miss S. Fry and Miss D. Hart
1955 Miss A. Mortimer and Miss J. A. Shilcock
Miss S. J. Bloomer and Miss P. E. Ward
1956 Miss A. Buxton and Miss A. Gibson
Miss F. Muller and Miss D. G. Seeney
1957 Miss A. Gibson and Miss D. R. Hard
Mrs. K. Hawton and Mrs. T. D. Long
1958 Miss M. E. Bueno and Miss A. Gibson
Mrs. W. du Pont and Miss M. Varner
1959 Miss J. Arth and Miss D. R. Hard
Mrs. J. G. Fleitz and Miss C. C. Truman
1960 Miss M. E. Bueno and Miss D. R. Hard
Miss S. Reynolds and Miss R. Schuurman
1961 Miss K. Hantze and Miss B. J. Moffitt
Miss J. Lehane and Miss M. Smith
1962 Miss B. J. Moffitt and Mrs. J. R. Susman
Mrs. L. E. G. Price and Miss R. Schuurman
1963 Miss M. E. Bueno and Miss D. R. Hard
Miss R. A. Ebbern and Miss M. Smith
1964 Miss M. Smith and Miss L. R. Turner
Miss B. J. Moffitt and Mrs. J. R. Susman
1965 Miss M. E. Bueno and Miss B. J. Moffitt
Miss F. Durr and Miss J. Lieffrig
1966 Miss M. E. Bueno and Miss N. Richey
Miss M. Smith and Miss J. A. M. Tegart
1967 Miss R. Casals and Mrs. L. W. King
Miss M. E. Bueno and Miss N. Richey
1968 Miss R. Casals and Mrs. L. W. King
Miss F. Durr and Mrs. P. F. Jones
1969 Mrs. B. M. Court and Miss J. A. M. Tegart
Miss P. S. A. Hogan and Miss M. Michel
1970 Miss R. Casals and Mrs. L. W. King
Miss F. Durr and Miss S. V. Wade
1971 Miss R. Casals and Mrs. L. W. King
Mrs. B. M. Court and Miss E. F. Goolagong
1972 Mrs. L. W. King and Miss B. F. Stove
Mrs. D. E. Dalton and Miss F. Durr
1973 Miss R. Casals and Mrs. L. W. King
Miss F. Durr and Miss B. F. Stove
1974 Miss E. F. Goolagong and Miss M. Michel
Miss H. F. Gourlay and Miss K. M. Krantzcke
1975 Miss A. Kiyomura and Miss K. Sawamatsu
Miss F. Durr and Miss B. F. Stove
1976 Miss C. M. Evert and Miss M. Navratilova
Mrs. L. W. King and Miss B. F. Stove
1977 Mrs. H. F. Gourlay Cawley and Miss J. C. Russell
Miss M. Navratilova and Miss B. F . Stove
1978 Mrs. G. E. Reid and Miss. W. M. Turnbull
Miss M. Jausovec and Miss V. Ruzici
1979 Mrs. L. W. King and Miss M. Navratilova
Miss B. F. Stove and Miss W. M. Turnbull
1980 Miss K. Jordan and Miss A. E. Smith
Miss R. Casals and Miss W. M. Turnbull
1981 Miss M. Navratilova and Miss P. H. Shriver
Miss K. Jordan and Miss A. E. Smith
1982 Miss M. Navratilova and Miss P. H. Shriver
Miss K. Jordan and Miss A. E. Smith
1983 Miss M. Navratilova and Miss P. H. Shriver
Miss R. Casals and Miss W. M. Turnbull
1984 Miss M. Navratilova and Miss P. H. Shriver
Miss K. Jordan and Miss A. E. Smith
1985 Miss K. Jordan and Mrs. P. D. Smylie
Miss M. Navratilova and Miss P. H. Shriver
1986 Miss M. Navratilova and Miss P. H. Shriver
Miss H. Mandlikova and Miss W. M. Turnbull
1987 Miss C. Kohde-Kilsch and Miss H. Sukova
Miss B. Nagelsen and Mrs. P. D. Smylie
1988 Miss S. Graf and Miss G. Sabatini
Miss L. Savchenko and Miss N. Zvereva
1989 Miss J. Novotna and Miss H. Sukova
Miss L. Savchenko and Miss N. Zvereva
1990 Miss J. Novotna and Miss H. Sukova
Miss K. Jordan and Mrs. P. D. Smylie
1991 Miss L. Savchenko and Miss N. Zvereva
Miss G. Fernandez and Miss J. Novotna
1992 Miss G. Fernandez and Miss N. Zvereva
Miss J. Novotna and Mrs. L. Savchenko-Neiland
1993 Miss G. Fernandez and Miss N. Zvereva
Mrs. L. Neiland and Miss J. Novotna
1994 Miss G. Fernandez and Miss N. Zvereva
Miss J. Novotna and Miss A. Sanchez Vicario
1995 Miss J. Novotna and Miss A. Sanchez Vicario
Miss G. Fernandez and Miss N. Zvereva
1996 Miss M. Hingis and Miss H. Sukova
Miss M.J. McGrath and Mrs. L. Neiland
1997 Miss G. Fernandez and Miss N. Zvereva
Miss N.J. Arendt and Miss M.M. Bollegraf
1998 Miss M. Hingis and Miss J. Novotna
Miss L.A. Davenport and Miss N. Zvereva

MIXED DOUBLES

Year	Winners	Year	Winners	Year	Winners
1913	Hope Crisp and Mrs. C. O. Tuckey		*F. A. Sedgman and Miss D. Hart*	1974	O. K. Davidson and Mrs. L. W. King
	J. C. Parke and Mrs. D. R. Larcombe	1949	E. W. Sturgess and Mrs. S. P. Summers		*M. J. Farrell and Miss L. J. Charles*
1914	J. C. Parke and Mrs. D.R. Larcombe		*J. E. Bromwich and Miss L. Brough*	1975	M. C. Riessen and Mrs. B. M. Court
	A. F. Wilding and Mlle. M. Broquedis	1950	E. W. Sturgess and Miss L. Brough		*A. J. Stone and Miss B. F. Stove*
1919	R. Lycett and Miss E. Ryan		*G. E. Brown and Mrs. P. C. Todd*	1976	A. D. Roche and Miss F. Durr
	A. D. Prebble and Mrs. Lambert Chambers	1951	F.A. Sedgman and Miss D. Hart		*R. L. Stockton and Miss R. Casals*
1920	G. L. Patterson and Mlle. S. Lenglen		*M. G. Rose and Mrs. N. M. Bolton*	1977	R. A. J. Hewitt and Miss G. R. Stevens
	R. Lycett and Miss E. Ryan	1952	F.A. Sedgman and Miss D. Hart		*F. D. McMillan and Miss B. F. Stove*
1921	R. Lycett and Miss E. Ryan		*E. Morea and Miss T. D. Long*	1978	F. D. McMillan and Miss B. F. Stove
	M. Woosnam and Miss P. L. Howkins	1953	V. Seixas and Miss D. Hart		*R. O. Ruffels and Mrs. L. W. King*
1922	P. O'Hara-Wood and Mlle. S. Lenglen		*E. Morea and Miss S. Fry*	1979	R. A. J. Hewitt and Miss G. R. Stevens
	R. Lycett and Miss E. Ryan	1954	V. Seixas and Miss D. Hart		*F. D. McMillan and Miss B. F. Stove*
1923	R. Lycett and Miss E. Ryan		*K. R. Rosewall and Mrs. W. du Pont*	1980	J. R. Austin and Miss T. Austin
	L. S. Deane and Mrs. D. C. Shepherd-Barron	1955	V. Seixas and Miss D. Hart		*M. R. Edmondson and Miss D. L. Fromholtz*
1924	J. B. Gilbert and Miss K. McKane		*E. Morea and Miss L. Brough*	1981	F. D. McMillan and Miss B. F. Stove
	L. .A. Godfree and Mrs. D. C. Shepherd-Barron	1956	V. Seixas and Miss S. Fry		*J. R. Austin and Miss T. Austin*
1925	J. Borotra and Mlle. S. Lenglen		*G. Mulloy and Miss A. Gibson*	1982	K. Curren and Miss A. E. Smith
	H. L. de Morpurgo and Miss E. Ryan	1957	M. G. Rose and Miss D. R. Hard		*J. M. Lloyd and Miss W. M. Turnbull*
1926	L. A. Godfree and Mrs. L. A. Godfree		*N.A. Fraser and Miss A. Gibson*	1983	J. M. Lloyd and Miss W. M. Turnbull
	H. Kinsey and Miss M. K. Browne	1958	R. N. Howe and Miss L. Coghlan		*S. Denton and Miss L. W. King*
1927	F. T. Hunter and Miss E. Ryan		*K. Nielsen and Miss A. Gibson*	1984	J. M. Lloyd and Miss W. M. Turnbull
	L. A. Godfree and Mrs. L. A. Godfree	1959	R. Laver and Miss D. R. Hard		*S. Denton and Miss K. Jordan*
1928	P. D. B. Spence and Miss E. Ryan		*N.A. Fraser and Miss M. E. Bueno*	1985	P. McNamee and Miss M. Navratilova
	J. Crawford and Miss D. Akhurst	1960	R. Laver and Miss D. R. Hard		*J. B. Fitzgerald and Mrs. P. D. Smylie*
1929	F. T. Hunter and Miss H. Wills		*R. N. Howe and Miss M. E. Bueno*	1986	K. Flach and Miss K. Jordan
	I. G. Collins and Miss J. Fry	1961	F. S. Stolle and Miss L. R. Turner		*H. P. Guenthardt and Miss M. Navratilova*
1930	J. H. Crawford and Miss E. Ryan		*R. N. Howe and Miss E. Buding*	1987	M. J. Bates and Miss J. M. Durie
	D. Prenn and Fraulein H. Krahwinkel	1962	N. A. Fraser and Mrs. W. du Pont		*D. Cahill and Miss N. Provis*
1931	G. M. Lott and Mrs L. A. Harper		*R. D. Ralston and Miss A. S. Haydon*	1988	S. E. Stewart and Miss Z. L. Garrison
	I. G. Collins and Miss J. C. Ridley	1963	K. N. Fletcher and Miss M. Smith		*K. Jones and Mrs. S. W. Magers*
1932	E. Maier and Miss E. Ryan		*R. A. J. Hewitt and Miss D. R. Hard*	1989	J. Pugh and Miss J. Novotna
	H. C. Hopman and Mlle. J. Sigart	1964	F. S. Stolle and Miss L. R. Turner		*M. Kratzmann and Miss J. M. Byrne*
1933	G. von Cramm and Fraulein H. Krahwinkel		*K. N. Fletcher and Miss M. Smith*	1990	R. Leach and Miss Z. L. Garrison
	N. G. Farquharson and Miss M. Heeley	1965	K. N. Fletcher and Miss M. Smith		*J. B. Fitzgerald and Mrs P. D. Smylie*
1934	R. Miki and Miss D. E. Round		*A. D. Roche and Miss J. A. M. Tegart*	1991	J. B. Fitzgerald and Mrs. P. D. Smylie
	H. W. Austin and Mrs D. C. Shepherd-Barron	1966	K. N. Fletcher and Miss M. Smith		*J. Pugh and Miss N. Zvereva*
1935	F. J. Perry and Miss D. E. Round		*R. D. Ralston amd Mrs. L. W. King*	1992	C. Suk and Mrs L. Savchenko-Neiland
	H. C. Hopman and Mrs. H. C. Hopman	1967	O. K. Davidson and Mrs. L. W. King		*J. Eltingh and Miss M. Oremans*
1936	F. J. Perry and Miss D. E. Round		*K. N. Fletcher and Miss M. E. Bueno*	1993	M. Woodforde and Miss M. Navratilova
	J. D. Budge and Mrs. S. P. Fabyan	1968	K. N. Fletcher and Mrs. B. M. Court		*T. Nijssen and Miss M. M. Bollegraf*
1937	J. D. Budge and Miss A. Marble		*A. Metreveli and Miss O. Morozova*	1994	T. A. Woodbridge and Miss H. Sukova
	Y. Petra and Mme. R. Mathieu	1969	F. S. Stolle and Mrs. P. F. Jones		*T. J. Middleton and Miss L. M. McNeil*
1938	J. D. Budge and Miss A. Marble		*A. D. Roche and Miss J. A. M. Tegart*	1995	J. Stark and Miss M. Navratilova
	H. Henkel and Mrs. S. P. Fabyan	1970	I. Nastase and Miss R. Casals		*C. Suk and Miss G. Fernandez*
1939	R. L. Riggs and Miss A. Marble		*A. Metreveli and Miss O. Morozova*	1996	C. Suk and Miss H. Sukova
	F. H. D. Wilde and Miss N. B. Brown	1971	O. K. Davidson and Mrs. L. W. King		*M. Woodforde and Mrs. L. Neiland*
1946	T. Brown and Miss L. Brough		*M. C. Riessen and Mrs. B. M. Court*	1997	C. Suk and Miss H. Sukova
	G. E. Brown and Miss D. Bundy	1972	I. Nastase and Miss R. Casals		*A. Olhovskiy and Mrs L. Neiland*
1947	J. E. Bromwich and Miss L. Brough		*K. G. Warwick and Miss E. F. Goolagong*	1998	M. Mirnyi and Miss S. Williams
	C. F. Long and Mrs. N. M. Bolton	1973	O. K. Davidson and Mrs. L. W. King		*M. Bhupathi and Miss M. Lucic*
1948	J. E. Bromwich and Miss L. Brough		*R. Ramirez and Miss J. S. Newberry*		

THE JUNIOR CHAMPIONSHIP ROLL

BOYS' SINGLES

Year	Winner	Year	Winner	Year	Winner	Year	Winner
1947	K. Nielsen (Denmark)	1960	A. R. Mandelstam (S.A.)	1973	W. Martin (U.S.A.)	1986	E. Velez (Mexico)
1948	S. Stockenberg (Sweden)	1961	C. E. Graebner (U.S.A.)	1974	W. Martin (U.S.A.)	1987	D. Nargiso (Italy)
1949	S. Stockenberg (Sweden)	1962	S. Matthews (G.B.)	1975	C. J. Lewis (N.Z.)	1988	N. Pereira (Venezuela)
1950	J. A. T. Horn (G.B.)	1963	N. Kalogeropoulos (Greece)	1976	H. Guenthardt (Switzerland)	1989	N. Kulti (Sweden)
1951	J. Kupferburger (S.A.)	1964	I. El Shafei (U.A.R.)	1977	V.A. Winitsky (U.S.A.)	1990	L. Paes (India)
1952	R. K. Wilson (G.B.)	1965	V. Korotkov (U.S.S.R.)	1978	I. Lendl (Czechoslovakia)	1991	T. Enquist (Sweden)
1953	W.A. Knight (G.B.)	1966	V. Korotkov (U.S.S.R.)	1979	R. Krishnan (India)	1992	D. Skoch (Czechoslovakia)
1954	R. Krishnan (India)	1967	M. Orantes (Spain)	1980	T. Tulasne (France)	1993	R. Sabau (Romania)
1955	M. P. Hann (G.B.)	1968	J. G. Alexander (Australia)	1981	M.W. Anger (U.S.A.)	1994	S. Humphries (U.S.A.)
1956	R. Holmberg (U.S.A.)	1969	B. Bertram (S.A.)	1982	P. Cash (Australia)	1995	O. Mutis (France)
1957	J. I. Tattersall (G.B.)	1970	B. Bertram (S.A.)	1983	S. Edberg (Sweden)	1996	V.Voltchkov (Belarus)
1958	E. Buchholz (U.S.A.)	1971	R. Kreiss (U.S.A.)	1984	M.Kratzmann (Australia)	1997	W. Whitehouse (South Africa)
1959	T. Lejus (U.S.S.R.)	1972	B. Borg (Sweden)	1985	L. Lavalle (Mexico)	1998	R. Federer (Switzerland)

BOYS' DOUBLES

Year	Winners	Year	Winners	Year	Winners
1982	P. Cash and J. Frawley	1988	J. Stoltenberg and T. Woodbridge	1994	B. Ellwood and M. Philippoussis
1983	M. Kratzmann and S.Youl	1989	J. Palmer and J. Stark	1995	M. Lee and J.M. Trotman
1984	R. Brown and R. Weiss	1990	S. Lareau and S. Leblanc	1996	D. Bracciali and J. Robichaud
1985	A. Moreno and J.Yzaga	1991	K. Alami and G. Rusedski	1997	L. Horna and N. Massu
1986	T. Carbonell and P. Korda	1992	S. Baldas and J. Draper	1998	R. Federer and O. Rochus
1987	J. Stoltenberg and T. Woodbridge	1993	S. Downs and J. Greenhalgh		

GIRLS' SINGLES

Year	Winner	Year	Winner	Year	Winner	Year	Winner
1947	Miss B. Domken (Belgium)	1960	Miss K. Hantze (U.S.A.)	1973	Miss A. Kiyomura (U.S.A.)	1986	Miss N. Zvereva (U.S.S.R.)
1948	Miss O. Miskova (Czechoslovakia)	1961	Miss G. Baksheeva (U.S.S.R.)	1974	Miss M. Jausovec (Yugoslavia)	1987	Miss N. Zvereva (U.S.S.R.)
1949	Miss C. Mercelis (Belgium)	1962	Miss G. Baksheeva (U.S.S.R.)	1975	Miss N.Y. Chmyreva (U.S.S.R.)	1988	Miss B. Schultz (Netherlands)
1950	Miss L. Cornell (G.B.)	1963	Miss D. M. Salfati (France)	1976	Miss N.Y. Chmyreva (U.S.S.R.)	1989	Miss A. Strnadova (Czechoslovakia)
1951	Miss L. Cornell (G.B.)	1964	Miss P. Bartkowicz (U.S.A.)	1977	Miss L. Antonoplis (U.S.A.)	1990	Miss A. Strnadova (Czechoslovakia)
1952	Miss ten Bosch (Netherlands)	1965	Miss O. Morozova (U.S.S.R.)	1978	Miss T. Austin (U.S.A.)	1991	Miss B. Rittner (Germany)
1953	Miss D. Kilian (S.A.)	1966	Miss B. Lindstrom (Finland)	1979	Miss M. L. Piatek (U.S.A.)	1992	Miss C. Rubin (U.S.A.)
1954	Miss V.A. Pitt (G.B.)	1967	Miss J. Salome (Netherlands)	1980	Miss D. Freeman (Australia)	1993	Miss N. Feber (Belgium)
1955	Miss S. M. Armstrong (G.B.)	1968	Miss K. Pigeon (U.S.A.)	1981	Miss Z. Garrison (U.S.A.)	1994	Miss M. Hingis (Switzerland)
1956	Miss A. S. Haydon (G.B.)	1969	Miss K. Sawamatsu (Japan)	1982	Miss C. Tanvier (France)	1995	Miss A. Olsza (Poland)
1957	Miss M. Arnold (U.S.A.)	1970	Miss S. Walsh (U.S.A.)	1983	Miss P. Paradis (France)	1996	Miss A. Mauresmo (France)
1958	Miss S. M. Moore (U.S.A.)	1971	Miss M. Kroschina (U.S.S.R.)	1984	Miss A. N. Croft (G.B.)	1997	Miss C. Black (Zimbabwe)
1959	Miss J. Cross (S.A.)	1972	Miss I. Kloss (S.A.)	1985	Miss A. Holikova (Czechoslovakia)	1998	Miss K. Srebotnik (Slovenia)

GIRLS' DOUBLES

Year	Winners	Year	Winners	Year	Winners
1982	Miss B. Herr and Miss P. Barg	1988	Miss J. A. Faull and Miss R. McQuillan	1994	Miss E. De Villiers and Miss E. E. Jelfs
1983	Miss P. Fendick and Miss P. Hy	1989	Miss J. Capriati and Miss M. McGrath	1995	Miss C. Black and Miss A. Olsza
1984	Miss C. Kuhlman and Miss S. Rehe	1990	Miss K. Habsudova and Miss A. Strnadova	1996	Miss O. Barabanschikova and Miss A. Mauresmo
1985	Miss L. Field and Miss J. Thompson	1991	Miss C. Barclay and Miss L. Zaltz	1997	Miss C. Black and Miss I. Selyutina
1986	Miss M. Jaggard and Miss L. O'Neill	1992	Miss M. Avotins and Miss L. McShea	1998	Miss E. Dyrberg and Miss J. Kostanic
1987	Miss N. Medvedeva and Miss N. Zvereva	1993	Miss L. Courtois and Miss N. Feber		